A LEADER'S Tripping POINTS

Guide to Cognizance

CORPORATE JUNGLE SERIES - 1

R V G KULKARNI

INDIA • SINGAPORE • MALAYSIA

Notion Press Media Pvt Ltd

No. 50, Chettiyar Agaram Main Road,
Vanagaram, Chennai, Tamil Nadu – 600 095

First Published by Notion Press 2021
Copyright © R V G Kulkarni 2021
All Rights Reserved.

ISBN 978-1-63745-491-6

This book has been published with all efforts taken to make the material error-free after the consent of the author. However, the author and the publisher do not assume and hereby disclaim any liability to any party for any loss, damage, or disruption caused by errors or omissions, whether such errors or omissions result from negligence, accident, or any other cause.

While every effort has been made to avoid any mistake or omission, this publication is being sold on the condition and understanding that neither the author nor the publishers or printers would be liable in any manner to any person by reason of any mistake or omission in this publication or for any action taken or omitted to be taken or advice rendered or accepted on the basis of this work. For any defect in printing or binding the publishers will be liable only to replace the defective copy by another copy of this work then available.

Dedicated to my mother

Smt. Vimala G Kulkarni

The epitome of love, humanity, hard work, sacrifice, and selflessness

Contents

Foreword	7
Author's Note	11
Acknowledgements	13
Preface	15
1. Leaders – The Beginning of Their End	21
2. Connecting Points: Brick and Mortar	26
3. Connecting Points: The Digital World	65
4. The New Lens to View	80
5. Deception Management	95
6. Skip Level Pitfalls	110
7. Change Agent for Managers	116
8. The Art of Managing Human Resources	123
9. Conclusion	137

Foreword

RVG Kulkarni hails from a small hamlet and had his education in vernacular medium in a government school followed by graduation in agricultural science and ending up with an MBA from a State University. Hard work and perseverance helped him do well in his chequered career. His decades of experience in different organizations from a government department to a traditional Indian bank followed by a next generation bank, coupled with deep interactions with several IT friends, has helped him paint a much bigger and more colourful picture of the corporate world in this first book.

It was a sheer delight to read this maiden book from my own student, RVG Kulkarni. I read the whole book in one go, with just one break – thanks to its sheer simplicity and the deeper and more complex insights of the corporate world explained in lucid terms. As I read through it, I was personally transported many times to various organizations I had worked for, and I could humorously connect to individuals I have met in my career and recollect their traits and behaviours, which are so nicely described in this book.

Spread over nine chapters, RVG Kulkarni drafts his journey in the corporate jungle, starting from the traditional government departments to new age banking. He deftly manoeuvres through the rigid government departments and describes lucidly the behaviour of subordinates and the matching responses of the bosses! He cautions the bosses against games played by different subordinates or juniors, with various examples on how dangerous these games can be.

RVG Kulkarni describes how – when 'brick and mortar' organizations have transformed to embrace the digital world in their workplace – people still play games of the older genre. The author also lists out current practices in organizations in great detail – like types of meetings, types of reviews, inquiries, audits and their pitfalls that the bosses need to look out for. He also gives solutions and details of precautions to be taken care of by the bosses.

The author's elaborate portion on town halls is not only educative, but also covers cruelly hilarious practices followed by subordinates in all kinds of organizations. His advice is a compulsory read for bosses in all organizations. Even though some suggestions read like normal dos and don'ts, these are pitfalls most of us do slip into. His details on managing call traffic, email traffic, social media, messages, VCs, and etiquettes is very educative.

Acknowledging the fact that the corporate jungle is fiercely competitive with managers playing games to survive, RVG Kulkarni goes much further than skin deep with his fluent understanding of the psychology of people. His classification of subordinates according to their orientation towards themselves and their organization is hardly covered in any MBA textbooks. One can easily classify most of our subordinates and can appreciate the greater detail into which the author has delved.

Chapter 8 of this book – covering the art of managing human resources – is a must read for all managers. This is a sort of summarizing chapter which tells all bosses how to manage the human resources available to him or her. The last chapter cannot hide the life science background of the author. This book is a must read for any manager in any organization – be it a bank, IT firm or a government department. The behaviour of a subordinate seems to be so predictably uniform, irrespective of the holding nature or domain area of the organization, which has been so nicely captured and seamlessly illustrated by RVG Kulkarni.

I must confess, I am very proud of RVG Kulkarni, who has been a very impressive student of mine. This book written by him is very lucid and I advise every manager or management student to read this. Bosses may like to keep it as a tool kit to be referred to at all times.

Foreword

Dr. M.S. Subhas

IIT (M), IIM (A)

Professor of Management,

Kousali Institute of Management Studies (KIMS)

Former Vice Chancellor, Vijayanagar Sri Krishnadevaraya University, Bellari, Karnataka.

Author's Note

Dr. M.S. Subhas holds a PhD in Management Studies from Karnataka University, PGDM from IIM-Ahmedabad and B. Tech, IIT Madras.

He is a member – Board of Governors, IIM Rohtak, and IIM Bengaluru, Chairman of BIC Society, Hubli, and Director of Best Practices Foundation, Dharwad. He has presented over 50 research papers in international and national journals. His proposal for a project based on MOVE, adopted for Paravets, was among the top proposals selected by World Bank among 1,700 proposals received all over the world. He also served as a vice chancellor of Vijayanagar Sri Krishnadevaraya University, Bellari.

His extraordinary knowledge, calibre, mastery over the subject, and his inimitable teaching techniques are comparable to the standards in any of the best business schools in the world. Thanks to IIT-M and IIM-A grooming, he brought the world of excellence to a management school in Karnataka University in Dharwad.

He epitomizes simplicity, honesty, integrity, razor-sharp focus, and brilliance – a very rare combination indeed.

I owe a lot to him, like many thousands of students, for inspiring, imparting the best education, and setting the highest benchmarks.

– R V G Kulkarni

Acknowledgements

I thank every person who worked as my boss, my colleague, and my support staff. I also thank every customer, dealer, distributor, friend, and relative who shared their experiences with their bosses and subordinates.

From the bottom of my heart, I remember my late mother, Smt. Vimala. Even after 36 years, she is an everlasting source of inspiration for my father, all family members, and me.

I would also like to sincerely thank my mother, Smt. Parimala, who took the dilapidated cradle of our broken home and slogged to build it selflessly.

My heartfelt thanks and salutations to my father, Shri. G. R. Kulkarni. In every creative world – be it music, dance, lyrics, and drama – he is an inspiration. He has published a collection of poems in Kannada named *Nichhala Niluvu* (Clear Stance) and was closely associated with the Kannada litterateur circle. Amongst them were Dr. D.R. Bendre and Dr. V.K Gokak (both Jnanapeetha awardees – the highest award in literature in India,) Dr. Betageri Krishna Sharma, And Dr R.S Mugali. My father has stood by me at every step like a rock and has

Acknowledgements

always encouraged me. I thank my in-laws, Mrs Sridevi and Mr. Srinivas Kulkarni, for their encouragement.

I also thank famous music director, Dr. Hamsalekha, also known as 'Nada Brahma' in the music industry, as well as well-known film director, Mr. Yograj Bhat, for their inspiration. My interactions with them – spread over several years – helped me to gain insights into their creative world and inspired me to write a book. I thank my friend and batchmate, Mr. V.C. Sajjanar, IPS, Commissioner of Police Cyberabad, Hyderabad, Telangana state. for his encouragement and support.

I thank my wife Rohini, son Aman, and daughter Aditi who are always pillars of strength for me and a perennial source of love, care, and affection.

I thank my sisters – Smt. Rajashree and her husband Mr. Shreenath and Smt. Bhagya and her husband Mr. Prasanna – for their love and affection, and my brother Shrikrishna (KK), my critic, and his wife Vidya for navigating and course correcting me whenever I was at crossroads while writing this book.

I thank the Notion Press Publications CEO Mr. Naveen, his team – Lakshmi, Vignesh, and Sarvesh – for helping me in editing, publishing, and marketing the book.

I also thank all my readers who have wholeheartedly encouraged me from day one.

Preface

I hail from Nesargi, a hamlet in Belagavi district, Karnataka. I went to the government school and studied in Kannada medium. I completed my B.Sc. in agriculture sciences and MBA in marketing from Karnataka University. Like any other small-town student, I faced many challenges and hurdles when I moved to bigger cities to pursue studies and to take part in competitive examinations. It was a herculean task. Yet I fought my way and cleared the Staff Selection Commission examination. I got the job of Inspector of Customs and Central Excise and worked for two years. I also simultaneously pursued the Indian Civil Services examination but missed narrowly in being selected. And then, I was selected as a Probationary Officer at a branch of Canara Bank. After working for close to six years in Canara Bank, I joined HDFC Bank Ltd, a new generation private bank.

These three organizations had completely different styles of management and work culture, and were set against completely different backdrops. It also gave me an opportunity to work under different types of leaders. I also was exposed to the games people play to showcase the best they have and conceal the reality. Many leaders could understand these games and managed them well, but many others were clueless. During my interactions with clients in various organizations – from pharma to the IT sector – I noted down such incidents where supervisors, and even senior management teams, were taken for a royal ride. It took me another few years to bridge all these pieces during weekends to compile them in the form of a book. These are not anecdotes, but ways and means people adopt to deceive their leaders. As a leader, if you have a single weakness, there are people who take just a few days to understand it and lay down a tripping point that you cannot avoid.

Every day, people interact with their boss more than their family members. Many times, this character – the boss – encroaches into our personal lives. For many, it haunts them and for some it motivates them. I have encountered very interesting, amazing people in my career as my leaders. I have learned many good things. I personally never evaluate my boss or brood on his/her negative traits. I believe that it is not my job. I do assess their behaviour and try to learn the very best qualities they have. This has helped me immensely to grow as a person and as a professional. I owe my success to each one of them.

Then why write a book on leaders and alert them on the several tripping points they need to be careful of? Is there a need to subject people to another onslaught of new management mantras? Well, while many of us know, what most of us have not realized is the fact that a leader always gets stage-managed behaviour. He seldom gets to know the truth. At the top of the pyramid, one is alone. Even if the emperor is naked, who will tell him? Instead, they tell him that he has the best attire in the world. Unfortunately, many believe that and feel proud of it. What one gets on the stage is a well-rehearsed drama where every act is manipulated. Every actor is a veteran. The stage is set, the screenplay is continuous, the dialogues are carefully written, the drama is well rehearsed and then the boss is made to sit in the audience. One tends to believe what one sees. What goes on behind the scenes, in the green room, is unknown. My attempt is to take you backstage and show you the reality. This is not an attempt to tarnish a genuine show and is not an attempt to sow the seeds of suspicion in every boss's mind but to enable them to differentiate genuine behaviour with that which is stage-managed.

As a leader, you get what you encourage. You encourage meritocracy, honesty, integrity, genuine performance, and operational efficiency – you get the same. If you encourage mediocracy, dishonesty, fake performance, and inefficiency – you get the same. There are many smart people who cover these negative traits, sugar coat them, and may offer them to you on a platter. This book will alert you for sure.

I was very fortunate to work under the most dynamic and the ablest, visionary leader who built a world-class bank from the scratch. It's none other than Mr. Aditya Puri. One of the reasons he was successful was because he never got carried away by anyone. He was crystal clear in his objectives and thought process and knew exactly what is in the best interest of the customers and the bank. His famous one-liner was, "Where are the *laddus?*" (A sweet delicacy, which is distributed in India after any success.) I have witnessed many presentations and town halls. If anyone ever tried to give elaborate plans, strategies and or a spice-filled story, he would ask, "That's fine, but where are the *laddus*? I do not see any results that can be quantified." Since then, no one ever tried to mislead him. One more one-liner that he used to use when I joined HDFC Bank in the year 2000 was, "This is English. I do not understand English. Explain it to me in simple Hindi." He would come with this punchline if anyone started beating around the bush with no clarity or started giving abbreviations, fancy names, etc. This one line would cut off all those MBA-style fancy presentations or the use of exotic terms to explain the process. These two sentences made the process simple and result oriented. No reasons and excuses were acceptable. No fancy names and jargons could mislead. Unfortunately, leaders in most of the organizations I have interacted with have never had such clarity of thoughts and simple solutions. In the last 28 years of my corporate life, I have seen – whether it is a small firm run by an individual or a huge organization – either stagnating or withering away due to weak management teams and mislead leaders.

Preface

It's my natural instinct to observe people. Be it at e airports, hotels, while traveling in India or abroad, I keep watching the behavioural part of a few typical characters I come across. These people are unique. I may not even speak to them. But I make sure to keep them in my memory and use them when I write stories or create a character in my scripts for films. It also helps me to know the local language, the culture, the history, and the heritage. Irrespective of the region or country, most of the behaviours do not change, but some of them change drastically and are unique to the specific region or country. Local customs/traditions always influence the way people behave. My stint in theatre during school and college days and my obsession with the subject of psychology makes everyone I see an interesting character to observe. I see them, analyse them, and match them with my previous experiences. I would always try to find out the root cause of one's reactions to a given situation. In the process, I have realized that it makes sense to be at your natural best. There is no point in 'stage managing' your behaviour all the time.

You cannot be thinking and acting in life. Let it be natural. But it should be well groomed and polished with all these years of learning, interacting with people, and having faced many challenges in life. The purpose of this book is to caution readers and bosses on the pitfalls people create. The trap they lay and how they lead you there must be known to you. While the whole world watches the boss jumping into the pit, the boss does not realize the same. In fact, he enjoys it.

Preface

We live in a fiercely competitive corporate world. One cannot avoid people playing games in a work environment. In fact, role-plays are a part of human life. We play various roles at any given point in time. We manipulate facts, try to create a 'feel good factor', and hide the truth. If boss is aware of these pitfalls, one can get to know the truth; one can avoid these well-laid traps and take suitable steps to manage the organization. Smart leaders would know what genuine behaviour is and what is cooked up. I have come across super smart managers behaving as if they are ignorant of the traps laid out, but they are very well aware of the reality. They let the subordinates play their games and, one fine day, they give them a piece of their mind. Probably they need not read this book. This book is also an attempt to let you know that it's better to exhibit what you are and not what you want to be, face the bitter reality, bite the bullet, and seek your supervisor's help to achieve the corporate objectives rather than living a stage-managed life. Never try to camouflage your natural behaviour. Hone it. Tone it. Polish it. But never lose your SELF. If I am able create a great working equation between the leader and his subordinate and make every leader understand various tripping points laid down by everyone so that he/she can avoid them, my purpose is served. I hope you will enjoy reading this book and correlate many incidents you would have experienced by now with those you come across here. If not, I am sure you will come across them soon. Happy reading.

CHAPTER 1

Leaders – The Beginning of Their End

A leader is the person who leads or commands a group, organization, or a country. A leader is a visionary, a motivator, and a great performer. Leaders thrive on paradox and oscillate between too much and too little control to ensure long-term effectiveness. They convey a grand design and navigate the company through troubled waters. They possess extraordinary product knowledge, understand processes, possess people development and talent management skills, and ensure they give the best products to the customers, create a happy work environment, and give the best return on investment for investors. They develop a system in order to groom people at all levels to ensure that organizations run professionally. They also ensure compliance to ethics and laws of the land. In today's world, leaders need not be at the top end of the hierarchy. They can be at a lower level of the pyramid. Anyone who supervises and manages a set of people below him or her is a leader. We also call him/her a boss.

Leaders also have a challenge in identifying the right talent and grooming them to execute their grand plans. They also have face cutthroat competition, and face challenges in cutting costs and increasing profits and market share. They also need to satisfy ever demanding and pampered customers as every market has turned into a buyer's market. Above all, they have limited time and resources to get results.

Leadership is a power centre. Power corrupts in many ways. As they can decide the future of all the people who report to them, people below them start manipulating the system. They will be waiting for one wrong move, one small window of opportunity to take the leader for a ride.

One of the factors which leads to the beginning of the end of glorious leaders is that of 'reality' never reaching the leader. It can be due to:

- arrogance
- a know-it-all attitude
- lack of patience and time
- tearing hurry to get quick results
- insecurity
- lack of long-term plans
- investor/shareholders' pressure.

No danger ever comes as a surprise. Nature always gives enough alerts. We ignore them. Similarly, many cues emanate and keep giving hints to the leaders. They treat them as routine matters, too small to give preference to and ignore them. The dangers then start snowballing and create an avalanche.

Arrogance is behaviour full of self-worth or self-importance of a person who says and shows that he/she has a feeling of superiority over others. Arrogance makes one not even listen to others. They will have their own version/judgement for every incident. People in such cases stop giving suggestions or ideas, and they toe the leader's line. Even if it is a wrong decision, they heap praises. But they never appreciate such leadership behaviour and nor do they implement any of the plans/ strategies thrust on them.

Many leaders think that if anyone doesn't toe the line, he/she is a rebel, and such acts are considered as acts of defiance and insubordination. At the same time, leaders cannot keep on seeking concurrence from everyone. They identify the concern areas, come up with solutions after consulting few staff or experts, and expect everyone to execute. It's a fine balancing act. But as a leader, one cannot be arrogant.

It is true that leaders know many things more than others. But every successful leader must have the habit of listening to and respecting others' views. Many leaders think that they are experts and have an attitude of "I know everything." Many times, they ridicule new ideas – which actually kills the creativity of the team and individuals.

For many leaders, their quarterly results are critical. They are in a hurry to get quick results. They want to impress the board and investors with the best results. They will never listen to anyone who gives ideas to build an organization in the long run. For them, quarterly top and bottom lines are critical.

Some have an extreme sense of insecurity. They put on a brave face, but they are cowards inside. They do not like any smart person working under them. They do not groom talent and always build a coterie who always applaud every decision taken by them.

Unlike family-owned businesses, not every person who works for companies as a professional has long-term plans. They have fixed tenures, and they want to get quick results, make some quick bucks, and hunt for newer opportunities somewhere. This is also augmented by investors/shareholders' pressure. They do not have time for building an organization on a long-term basis.

All the above and many more reasons lead to the beginning of the end of a leader and, many times, the organization. It gives the best possible opportunity for people in the organization who only capitalize on every available opportunity to carpet the leader's path with numerous tripping points. Even if a leader trips, he/she doesn't realize, as they believe that they can never fail. The 'make to believe' trap laid by everyone makes the journey look smooth for them. Every fall is on a soft cushion of comfort and hence the leader doesn't get hurt. In fact, they don't even realize. By the time they realize and fix the issues, it may be too late. If leaders listen, aim to build a long-lasting organization, have ethics and moral responsibilities, and have no weaknesses whatsoever, then subordinates will have no chance to create tripping points.

In the subsequent chapters, we will look at how people trip a leader, how leaders can take adequate precautions, etc.

CHAPTER 2

Connecting Points: Brick and Mortar

In spite of the digital era, we keep connecting with people in our office. The following are the main connecting points between you and your subordinates. Some precautions that you need to take at all these connecting points are covered.

The workplace

Gone are the days when we had typical manufacturing units where white and blue-collar staff would chug out for several hours under challenging working conditions. There were separate recreation clubs for different classes of staff and employee welfare societies running a provision store that offered discounts was a luxury. Today, the workplace is different. Even manufacturing units these days are swanky and modern.

Most of the office spaces are air-conditioned and there is hardly any physical drudgery. Barring a few sectors like construction sites, mining, and infrastructure related sectors, the work environment is pretty decent and conducive. But it is the mental battle that creates a separate war zone in everyone's mind. That's the problem.

We have more repetitive syndromes due to hours being spent at the desk. With laptops, iPads, and email accessibility on the mobile, virtually every place is a workplace. VC and audio bridges can get you connected with people across the globe. People have their front-end office in one part of the globe and backend operations and head office in another part. Time zones are different. It's tough to attend VCs and meetings at odd hours. So, the workplace is not a brick-and-mortar structure. It's everywhere. Hence, your boss can connect with you anytime, anywhere. Earlier once people left the office, it was tough to get connected. Imagine those days where landlines were a luxury and very few staff would have a mobile. Once they left office, it was tough to call them even when there was an emergency. Today your boss can trace you anywhere. With Face Time and VCs, you cannot even hide your feelings. So, it is tough for the subordinates to escape their bosses, and yet every boss will face the challenge of getting his work done without infringing the privacy of his staff. He also needs to comply with the rules of the organization – some organizations have rules where one cannot disturb the staff after office hours unless it is an emergency situation.

It makes sense to have a cordial and trouble-free relationship with your boss, whether you work in a brick-and-mortar office or a virtual office. It makes sense if communication between the staff is open to resolve an issue, get more sales, and comply with processes rather than settle scores and win battles one after another for the sake of one-upmanship.

Ensure that you choose a place where you can have a bird's eye view of the office. Most of the office layouts have a corner room or cabin for the boss. But it is better to choose a place where you can see your staff without too much of an issue. Ideally, one must know about the absenteeism or travel plans of your staff. You should also share your weekly itinerary, including travel plans. It helps to avoid unimportant communications to each other while on leave or travel.

You need to meet your team for following reasons:

- Planned Meetings
- Unplanned Meetings (Casual Drops),
- Reviews
- Crisis Handling

Planned meetings

Are meetings necessary? Please assess. Meetings are important but not critical. If you want to convey an important decision or want to directly ask for a feedback on an important strategy or to discuss a crisis situation, schedule a meeting. Many people believe that series of meetings in a day makes their day. They hop from one meeting room to another and keep themselves extremely busy. Their breakfast, lunch, evening snacks, dinner, and intermittent snacks, etc, are done on the meeting table. With multiple tasks on everyone's table, it's now inevitable to strongly convey the message only through personal meetings. Earlier one simple official circular would suffice, but now meetings and multiple follow-ups are needed to convey a simple message. Over-communication has become the new norm. Have planned meetings far and few and only for very important issues. The best way to evaluate the effectiveness of the meeting is to think for a minute after the meeting is over and jot down what the outcome was. Was it useful? If not, do not conduct such meetings in future.

If you want your team to come prepared for the meeting, please share an agenda well in advance so that they come prepared. Involve all stakeholders. There will be instances where, midway through the meeting, one may realize that key personnel from other departments were not invited. To avoid last minute hassles, call all key stakeholders.

Start the meeting on time. In India, most of the meetings start late and people assume that there will be a delay. Nowadays, there is much more discipline and people have a better sense of time.

Brief your team on the purpose of the meeting. Come straight to the point. Discuss every point on the agenda. Beware of hijackers. We once assembled to discuss locations to be finalized for new branches. After 30 minutes into the meeting, we were discussing a political issue in a neighbouring state. No one knew who hijacked the meeting. Obviously, it was a person who had not identified any locations for branch expansion. The best way for him was to introduce a hot topic for discussion. Sometimes they will remind you of your childhood/ college days (nostalgic hijack), awards won by you (recognition hijack), your family members' talent (emotional hijack), your religious preferences (Atmic hijack, would we say?). Please have some anti-hijack alert systems in your mind and stick to the point. Do not allow anyone to hijack your meeting.

Let one of the members or your secretary record the minutes of the meeting. It should ideally have details of the meeting, tasks to be handled by key persons, support needed from other units, items to be escalated, and then a timeline to meet again to do a review if needed. Check the minutes of the meeting properly before sharing with all team members. The next meeting must be in continuation of the previous meeting to take stock of the situation and take some course correction measures. Then meetings become meaningful.

Unplanned meetings (Casual drops)

Make sure that your office cabin is not like a shop in a vegetable market – where anyone can walk in and spend some time. Have enough window blinds to keep off unwarranted staff who would be waiting to gate crash if you lift your head and make the slightest eye contact. If you are in a regional/head office, you will see many staff members from other locations and other departments who hang around in the lobby. They drop in casually and rob your time.

Please plan your day and stick to it. If need be, have a meeting at a common meeting room instead of your cabin. In case of delays, you can excuse yourself and come out. But it would be rude if you ask someone to leave your cabin midway.

In some cases, your staff may want to have a meeting with you. Please understand the purpose for which your staff want to meet you. Do they set an agenda and come? Do they just drop in? You may not be able to avoid these unscheduled visitors. You may even end up meeting unscheduled customers if you are in a service industry.

In most cases of unplanned visits, casual drop-ins are a complete waste of time for you. At the end, you would know they had a hidden agenda. Please ask them to come to the point straightaway rather than beating around the bush. Please stick to the agenda if you have to meet them.

I had a staff member who would drop in and first start a conversation on an issue in the company. He would elaborate on how he had solved it after lot of effort. Or he would inform me about various activities done at various companies followed by future activity plans. Then he would ask for leave by clubbing a couple of holidays. Next time when he walked into my cabin, I did not allow him to speak and instead, I asked him how many days leave he needed and asked him to apply online and move on. He smiled and asked me how come I had guessed!

Reviews

As the word suggests reviews are always a formal assessment of something, with the intention of instituting change if necessary. Synonymous with review are:

- Analysis
- Evaluation
- Assessment
- Investigation or probe
- Scrutiny
- Inquiry
- Exploration or an audit

Carry your own database/MIS when you review your staff or get the data from the authentic source. In most of the reviews, there is no time for cross-checking the information/facts/MIS. Share the yardsticks and parameters against which you want to review. Some supervisors send the format for presentation, including the sequence of slides, so that there is a uniformity. Having a sequence will help you focus on extremely important points first followed by the not so relevant ones.

The biggest misleading factor in reviews is presenting feel-good factors and information that is far from the reality. Instead of presenting what is the actual performance vis a vis targets, some have the habit of giving information on the scope available in the catchment area, potential for business, and so on. In many such reviews, even the senior and most experienced head of the division will always get misled by such tactics. They will start narrating the scope available for sales in a specific market instead of covering actual performance against the targets. They may also narrate how they would assign the work to every person and track them to get the results. This one piece of information could hijack the whole review process. This information is available in the public domain. No one would check what the actual performance is. When the next review happens, no one would remember what was discussed. Poor performance gets camouflaged by such misleading information. So, stick to your agenda.

Some make a huge vision statement before the presentation is made. Some coin a new caption like 'focused locations', 'cluster bombing', 'carpet bombing', 'marketing blitzkrieg', and so on. They never cover what was the actual business clinched, what the future business potential is, and when they will achieve their targets.

During the review or otherwise, some have the habit of sharing photographs with clients where a bouquet is given or a memorandum is exchanged. Some share the newspaper clippings. Most of the time, they share the potential business opportunities. These are really great efforts, and one must appreciate them. But reward only those who get results.

As a leader and a manager, know your people, geography, product, competition, new entrants, and market share details. Analyse competition and then arrive at how much more one can get the business. One cannot go by the MIS alone. Please keep a tab on such hijacking tactics or feel-good factors.

Please do not cancel planned meetings and reviews at the last minute unless there are emergency situations. I must share some feedback I used to get in some government departments. Unlike earlier days, now all government departments conduct serious meetings and reviews. Their meetings last at times for the whole day. A deputy collector's meetings and reviews spread across at least a day, as they discuss every developmental activity. They also get emergency calls and hence some deviations from the schedule are inevitable as per the nature of their job. In one of the states, a minister would call all the key officials for a review meeting to one location. Just before the commencement of the meeting, he would call it off due to some political emergency, as the minister would travel to another location. So the review meeting would be postponed to the next day and all would make arrangements for their stay. The next day, the minister would arrive late in the evening and then announce that since he had other critical appointments, the meeting was called off and they would be called in a few days. The entire top brass of administrators and executives would travel back to their locations. After a day, they would be again being called for a review meeting. This was almost a routine affair. In private organizations, such events may be very rare and unheard of. But this can happen in some government organizations and here no one can raise concerns, as they are governed by strict hierarchy and protocol. But they all became immune to this particular minister's meetings. They would also cancel their schedules and relax. It also started affecting the entire administrative and executive decision-making process. This was never noticed by the concerned ministers. Needless to say, the next election results were disastrous.

Analysis

Analysis is the detailed examination of the elements or structure of something. Analysis of raw data or even structured MIS is a serious business. One must evaluate the source of data or MIS. Today some people believe that whatever they get on the internet is authentic and reliable. It may not be. During the review of data or MIS, if the source of information is unreliable, the entire exercise is a waste. Once it is confirmed that the data is reliable, please check what you do with the same. What is the end use of it? If it is an internal database, usually given by the data analytics, check what the parameters were on which the data was culled out. Many times, one would not even know these parameters. Many data analytics may not have the practical information that is needed when they deal with the retail customer segment, which is mostly heterogeneous and dynamic. Even before you conduct a review with the front-end staff on the effectiveness of the database, do some litmus tests. Ask the ablest staff to make some calls or meet the customer and see the response. This needs to be done before the data is downloaded to all the staff. Instead of spending time on implementing across locations, one must do a litmus test, see its impact and then implement.

Focus on actual results. Here the review must end with what is working and what is not working. Some staff thrust data that may highlight one of their success stories. As a boss, you may not like frank feedback. So everyone would come with one success story, which you can never cross verify. Check the impact of the entire data rather than getting carried away by one success story. If you do so, the whole team ends up working on a dead database, resulting in waste of time, money, and energy. Next time, even if a genuinely good database is given the staff will not work and keep on fooling the whole system by sharing a one-off success story.

Evaluation

Evaluation is making a judgement about the amount, number, or value of something. If you are doing a review to evaluate, say, an impact of a marketing activity, use various analytical tools. Check how many leads were generated during the activity and whether any means were adopted to check the leads generated and converted. Many times, the photo of an event with some 400 customers or picture of customers thronging your activity desk are shown. It would give an excellent impression. Good advertisements may not end up in the sale of a product. Check why the marketing or promotional activity was conducted. Was it just to create awareness or to increase sales? If it was to create only awareness, check how many customers are aware of the product after the campaign and compare with the product awareness before the campaign. In each of these cases, there must be a mechanism to assess the actual impact by way of increased awareness or sales.

In banking, there is always a tussle between the customer, sales staff, loan sanctioning authority, and independent evaluators when it comes to evaluating the fair market price of the property to be mortgaged. Customers always take more than actual market value. Property valuation team and credit buyers take the actual registration value, which is very low. Another risk is that the value of the property would be very low when it is sold under stress. Reviews on property valuations never end with unanimity. One must have a fair knowledge of the area. Your network and knowledge of general property values in each area matters here. One must check the value of the properties sold in the area, visit the site, check the location, access road, elevation, structure of the property, vintage, and evaluate the materials used for construction. Collect this information before you do an evaluation. If you have this this information/knowledge, no one can take you for a ride and you will be able to convince either a customer or credit buyer or both.

Before any new product launch, ensure that all possible information/data is collected – products from the competition, their success rate, analysis of the target customer segment. The product must also be backed up by proper marketing strategies. The front-end staff must understand the product, its USP, salient features, and be able to sell it to those who need it. Many times, in the service industry, the terms and conditions associated with the product would be too many or would be complicated. If you are the decision-making authority, ensure that you collect the above information, evaluate the product, and ensure that the staff and the customers understand the product easily. The best way to judge a product is to get into the shoes of the customer. Would you genuinely buy the product if you were a customer? Ask your family for frank feedback. You know they are the best critics and judges.

The same strategy is applicable to the evaluation of marketing strategies before they are launched.

The evaluation process would be meaningful only when you know what is being evaluated, what information is needed, and whether the source of information is reliable. You may even take the help of experts to arrive at a suitable decision. But do involve everyone in the entire process, as these are very critical for the organization and will have long-term impact.

Assessment

Assessment is the action of assessing someone or something. For example, selection of staff for promotion or salary correction. We need to have a fair assessment.

For assessment, you need to get all the information – like vintage of the staff, years in the same role/ grade, the last few years' ratings, year of last promotion, staff related actions/memos if any, etc. If you are a part of this process, get every possible parameter used by the human resources (HR) department. Go through the list of staff and shortlist. Seek the opinion of your staff and collect and evaluate upward feedback on the short-listed candidates. If you do not have complete information, you may end up promoting people who do not deserve it. Ensure that assessment is done 100 percent fairly, with no bias on caste, colour, creed, region, religion, etc. Not only in India, but also in other countries, you will find prejudices and favouritism based on race, religion, gender, etc. One must also be a keen observer of your subordinates' lifestyles and opinions on their socio-religious aspects. You will come across a few staff members who have very strong prejudices and can be religious fanatics in recruiting and promoting staff who belong to their own caste/region/religion/state. This will kill professionalism and create an organization that has mediocre performers. It also leads to group-ism and favouritism. You cannot be a party to it unknowingly or inadvertently.

The assessment system of staff for promotion at lower levels is very systematic and organized. As one goes up in the ladder in many organizations, it is how well you get linked to the top management that matters. During my research on this topic, I have come across, in many organizations, that the most connected, manipulative staff end up taking the top slots. Somehow, the top management turns a Nelson's eye on merit. They also see more of comfort zones. These zones are created when they have people down below who always create a comfort zone for them. For every decision they just say, "Yes Sir/Yes Madam." These are the people who never handle challenging roles. They never do any work that makes them accountable. Their sole job is to impress the top management.

I once visited the corporate office of a company for business purposes and spent a lot of time with a key decision maker. He was a bit upset, and was discussing how people manipulate and never miss any opportunity.

He elaborated further that he was with one senior resource, known for manipulations, in an elevator in the corporate office a few months back. The head of HR entered the same elevator. In no time, the person switched the topic of conversation and said, "Oh My God. Can you believe managing the entire workload with over 100 people who are just new and then personally checking every parameter across ten departments? Can you see my swollen eyes? I leave office at 10 pm and carry home the workload and work up to 12 am and then again come back at 8.30 am in the morning. That's why I am paying a bomb to have a rented home close to office to reduce my travel time." And then, "Oh sorry sir, I did not notice you (looking at the HR head)." Naturally, the head of HR was amazed with this conversation and gave a thumbs up sign and left. The day I visited the corporate office, the guy was celebrating his promotion. Here the staff member assessed himself cleverly and created an impression that was difficult to erase.

Each role in the organization needs different skillsets. At a lower level, it is more about knowing the product/process or a specific program language in IT/BPO/KPO-related organizations.

Staff in the middle management level need to have better domain knowledge/mentoring/coaching/supervisory skills. They need to spend lot of time in honing the skills of their staff and monitoring them.

The top management needs to have a vision for the company. They must never compromise on ethics and moral values. They need to have zero tolerance on deviant behaviour against the core objectives of the organization. They must have a grand design for the organization. They must be much above the petty politics and games people play. They must keep their self-interests aside and work for the clients and the organization. They must build leadership at every level and keep at bay undeserving people. They need to have an extraordinary sense of vision and should be able to navigate the organization in good and turbulent times. They should be able to anticipate every opportunity to grow the organization organically or inorganically. They should possess a fair amount of product knowledge and should take every possible step to take on the competition. They must be extraordinary in communication and motivational skills. They must never keep their self-interest first. The interest of the customers should be at the top followed by that of the organization. They must never work in silos. They must know the art of coordination and cooperation. They need to be well connected in the industry. They must have a flair for new technology and should keep abreast of new technology. They need to be very good in resolving problems. They cannot be playing devil's advocate for every new initiative nor follow the culture of 'yes boss'. They must evaluate every new initiative, study the larger impact, take them up with stakeholders for support, and then implement. In short, they need to have every possible character of a true leader and a manager. These traits are to be evaluated with facts and figures and also the leadership qualities they exhibit over a period of time.

Unfortunately, movement of staff from one level to another level doesn't assess their core competency levels. Some organizations rely purely on performance/MIS and some on the vintage of staff and other feel-good factors. In many sales-oriented organizations, what finally matters is sales, and those working at the backend operations never ever get recognized even though they play key roles. Those who are good at sales (basically owing to their own calibre and skills) fail to perform when it comes to supervising people.

I have seen excellent sales staff ending up as the worst supervisors due to a lack of people management/

supervisory skills. The assessment process must ensure that people are evaluated on every parameter needed to occupy the next level.

It is imperative that skillsets needed at each level need to be identified. HR and line functions must groom staff to acquire skillsets that are needed at the next level.

Investigation/Probe

An investigation or a probe is the action of investigating someone or something. It is a formal enquiry or study. An investigation or a probe can be regarding some serious complaint against a staff member by another staff member, other unit heads, dealers, distributors, or a customer. In banking, it can also be centrally monitored triggers where some suspicious transaction is noticed in the accounts held by the staff member. In other sectors, it can be an insider trading allegation, whistle blower complaints, serious allegations of fraud/malpractices, allegations of harassment/favouritism, nexus with dealers/distributors/customers, allegations of pass backs, and so on.

Once you take charge of the department or a unit, please look for many triggers or indicators when you interact with your staff, customers, dealers, and distributors. Professionally run organizations will have checks and balances. They also will have very strict codes of conduct and terms and conditions associated with employment. Unfortunately, no staff looks at these terms. Please make sure that ethical codes of conduct are in place and all staff are very well aware of them. Many staff go overboard to do favours and try to impress you with expensive gifts to you and your family members on birthdays, arranging local travel, etc. As you know, nothing in this world comes free and there is no reason for any subordinate to spend money, time, and energy on you. While it's part of some cultures – where sweets/gifts are exchanged during festive seasons – be careful if they are too frequent, too expensive, and are followed by asking for any favours.

In the banking industry, investigations are ordered if a cheque issued by the staff gets bounced and if many transactions (more than the salary drawn by the staff) are noted. Investigations are also ordered if there are violations of insider trading norms, where one does trading in the stock of the company during the moratorium period. If you are meeting your staff for these purposes, you must know the background of the case. You should ask for an explanation from the concerned staff. You should also cross verify the details given vis a vis probe parameters. There are instances where the explanation given by the staff is forwarded without verifying the facts. Many staff indulge in non-compliance due to lack of awareness and some do it deliberately. One must know the difference and deal with it suitably.

In case of violation of any insider trading norms and other serious offenses, one must hand over the case to ER/HR team and mark these cases to the legal team as well.

In case of a probe into sexual harassment cases, please hand over the case to organization's internal sexual harassment committee. One must also collect substantial material and documentary evidence and then take a decision. In some organizations, I have come across false allegations and, in many cases, genuine complaints get lost due to an unprofessional and inefficient investigation team. As a leader, one must ensure – through fact-based investigation – and ensure justice to the staff.

Many times, these allegations are hushed up and silenced for the fear of damage to the reputation of the organization. This must never be done. If staff come to know that the organization will try to cover up such lapses, it encourages more people to indulge in such acts, leading to a total breakdown.

All companies have whistle blower policies, and these are investigated by an independent team. They collect testimonies from colleagues, superiors, and subordinates of the staff in question. Here, many times, the staff's boss feels that any negative remarks against his subordinates will tarnish his/her image. So, one tends to manipulate and rig the whole process of investigation. They warn the staff not to give any negative testimonies. They even dictate the script and ensure that the investigation does not implicate the staff. Such acts further erode the confidence of the staff members and encourage people to indulge in unlawful acts with more impunity. If you are part of such investigations, you must know how to extract the truth from the staff. One can easily come across a lot of circumstantial and documentary evidence to get the truth.

I have come across in many companies' people in key positions floating companies in the name of family members and friends who carry out work for the company. In one cement company, many top management staff had created transport companies in the name of very distant family members. They would manage these companies and get every possible benefit. Many of the IT company staff run parallel cab services and some even have a nexus with every possible service provider – from travel agents and transporters to housekeeping – and get maximum tangible and intangible benefits. If there are any probes/investigations into these matters, one must get to the bottom of it and unearth the blatant misuse of power.

In some small MNCs, they hand over the reins to the local staff and they believe that they would professionally manage the company. But in connivance with even top management, they empty the coffers. I have witnessed such events where MNCs later ordered a probe, filed FIRs, and then slowly wound up the operations. Such acts of mistrust will risk the reputation of the country, leading to less foreign investments. So MNCs must have independent audits at frequent intervals and have strict control on cost management.

In a few companies, they also keep track of the lifestyles of their staff. If the staff start leading a lifestyle far more than their known sources of income, it is a trigger to start probing. In one of the banks, a front-end sales staff was enjoying a lavish lifestyle. The branch manager was smart enough to spot this and informed his higher-ups. On probing, it was learnt that he used to run a parallel chit fund and money lending business, taking commissions from customers who availed loans, and had political links. He was promptly sacked.

In all cases of investigation/probe, every possible data/evidence must be collected and used for nailing the concerned staff. Many times, these can be challenged in a court of law. Hence, it is important to collect evidence. The company must also identify the lapses in the system and plug them immediately and send a revised process to all the staff straightaway. One must also carry out frequent training programs only to highlight the acts that would lead to suspension/ termination.

If you are a part of the investigating team, please ensure that you know the law of the land first, the internal policies and parameters of the company, and the full facts of the case, and then conduct an impartial investigation with no prejudices, favours, or preconceived notions. Verify facts/documents/data/information, etc, and interpret them correctly. Ensure that a fair report is submitted to the concerned person. It is better if you also cover the process lapses so that the organization can roll out a revised process to ensure that such incidents never recur in future. One must note that people will spread enough tripping points at every stage of investigation to mislead the same and if one is alert, one can navigate these traps easily.

Scrutiny

Scrutiny is the careful and detailed examination of something in order to get information about it. Scrutiny is when you look at something really closely – like when you are checking an answer sheet for mistakes.

Usually scrutiny of documents, database, or MIS is done in order to get the correct information. Here the source of data must be ascertained. If the data is from an authentic source, the information derived would also be authentic. In one of the IT companies, there was a practice of submitting fake bills. There was no cross verification either by the supervisor or the finance team. In some organizations, alcohol consumption by the staff is not allowed and is illegal during official travels. Some tend to get food bills in lieu of alcohol. Such bills are passed without scrutiny. With digital approval systems, physical bills are never scrutinized. In one company, in such an instance, careful examination revealed that the food bills included were for at least seven people when only one staff member had travelled. There are instances of consumption of diesel for generator sets running into lakhs of rupees for huge premises, as there was no control or scrutiny of the bills. Subcontracts in many companies are given by staff members to their close relatives – much against the company rules.

There are frauds while hiring people. There was an instance in an organization where, if you referred a person, you would get a cash reward in the form of a month's salary. Those on the selection panel would not be eligible for the cash reward nor could they refer anyone. So, one member of the selection panel would ask junior staff to refer the candidates and share the cash reward. None in HR or finance could get suspicious as to why only one or two staff members were referring candidates while others were not. So, if any approval comes on to your table and you are reviewing the same, please be alert and scrutinize the same thoroughly and, if need be, investigate or probe. During your discussions with your team, make them know that you check the bills/recommendations thoroughly before approving. This will act as a deterrent.

Inquiry

Inquiry is the act of asking for information. Unlike enquiry, where just information is required, in case of an inquiry, an investigation is held. The same principle, as explained earlier, holds good.

Exploration/Audit

Exploration is the act of exploring an unfamiliar area. It is an act of searching for the purpose of discovery of information or resources. In every organization, it is not uncommon to go for lateral hiring at middle management and senior levels. This is not an easy job. If you are part of this exercise, apart from collecting information from the hiring agency, collect market information. In any industry, it is common to have staff moving from one organization to another. You have to make informal very discrete enquiries. I have witnessed staff who committed a fraud in one organization end up getting plum posts in another. Some with serious sexual harassment cases get into another relatively new sector and get a job. At a national level, there is a need to have a repository of information/data on people who have been accused of or convicted for serious frauds/sexual harassment/insider trading, etc, so that other organizations do not end up hiring them. One must also do a referral check with the existing organization.

Skillsets at the middle and top management levels are the same and the present trend is to hire from completely unknown industries. I have seen bankers joining the IT industry and vice versa; people from banking getting into infrastructure and the hospitality industry, and from other sectors to banking and FMCGs. More than the knowledge of the product and processes, please explore people management skills, which are more critical and important. Even with in the industry, the organizational culture, norms, processes, and products change. Explore candidates who have the skillsets and behaviours that match your organization. When you interview such candidates, do not get carried away by the examples and stories they narrate. Many times, they distract the interviewer with stories and topics they are familiar with. Ask them to get to the point. Avoid candidates referred by influential third parties unless they deserve the job on their own merits. Record all your observations when you conduct an interview and select or reject a candidate.

Audit is also an official inspection of an organization's accounts, typically by an independent body. Audit reviews and discussions are usually unpleasant. In banking or any regulated financial sector, the front-end staff works on a razor edge. If they follow the process and insist on extra documentation or compliance from the customer, they could lose business. Some documentation and compliances cannot be deferred nor can they be approved with exceptions. If the process is violated and the customer is accommodated to get business or to retain the existing business, it would end up violating the internal guidelines and thus invite the wrath of audit team. At times, it may also lead to frauds.

As the head of the department, you also will have to maintain a balancing act when it comes to defending the process lapse or debating with the audit team. Please check the complete facts of the case. Check how the auditors came up with such negative observations. Were they based on the documentary evidence or facts?

In your discussion with them, please check what the law says or what the internal circular/guidelines say. Please ask your team to understand the guidelines first and check against the audit observations. If there is scope for any debate, prepare all the points that may help the discussion. Do not depend upon oral confirmations of compliance given by the staff. Do not forward the same without proper verification. Also, check what the impact of the non-compliance is. If it is hurting customer service, or results in reprimands by regulatory bodies or hurts the image of the company, one should have zero tolerance. One must also analyse and understand the circumstances that led to the lapses. The lapses can be due to lack of understanding of the process by the staff, especially those who have joined newly or joined from other departments or organizations. In such an event, one must arrange for a comprehensive training and awareness program. Ideally, every office must have mix of experienced and new staff to balance it out.

In the service industry, many times pressure from the boss or customers results in non-compliance. As a boss, you must know where and when to take a business call. The recommendations from your staff must be crisp but must cover key points. Send a bullet point format to your subordinates while seeking various approvals. Staff should send the details as per format, which will help you to take the right decision. If you rely on vague information and approve critical decisions, you will end up in big trouble.

People working in government department come under tremendous pressure from their seniors, influential businessmen, and powerful politicians to take deviations.

It can be for hiring a staff to giving a contract to their known people or hiring premises for business expansion, etc. In many cases, as a boss, you will not have access to information, nor will there be any internal guidelines. But things can go wrong any time. I have seen people at general manager and above level getting suspended or dismissed just a few days before their retirement due to a few wrong decisions they had taken years ago. And one must remember that one may be taking such decisions every day, day in and day out. It is also advisable to stick to the delegation matrix. In case of any ambiguity, consult your seniors.

In many cases, even experienced staff violate the processes knowingly. They do so by forging documents/signatures in order to avoid an audit remark. One must respect the audit remarks and take suitable action. It is also true that some overenthusiastic auditors try to entice staff to make mistakes. They first create a fear about non-compliance of a process, then hide a few documents that are critical. Many staff fall prey to it and forge the documents. The acts of enticing and cajoling staff to make mistakes must be dealt with seriously and they must be escalated to the audit head. However, staff must also be trained to accept lapses, if any, and rectify them later rather than resorting to forgery. In all these events, as a boss one must be extremely carefully.

In banking, all critical transactions are entered in the system and reports gets downloaded. The physical transaction slips are then verified with system-generated reports. In some organizations, the reports getting downloaded from the system can be altered/modified. This needs to be addressed by the IT team. They must ensure that no one is able to alter any report downloaded from the system. One can imagine the consequences if the very basis on which transactions are verified is forged.

Crisis handling

Crisis handling is another reason why you meet your staff. A crisis is a time of intense difficulty or danger. Your meeting can be to list out difficult or dangerous situations that may emanate or handle the ones that are already impacting the organization.

During urban cyclonic threats which hit the coastal parts of South India a few years ago, many organizations conducted meetings to list out precautionary measures to be adopted to face the natural calamity, but they never ever imagined the consequences of a cyclone. Most of them did not prepare well due to their inability to comprehend or imagine the seriousness of the situation. As a boss, do not get mislead by ill-prepared staff. Make your own study. Understand the gravity of the issue and prepare a disaster management plan. One must also involve other departments and organizations and coordinate with them in order to avoid or minimize the damage. A few decades ago, there was a serious earthquake in the central part of India. Apart from taking various measures to help the affected people, the first thing the Minister of the

Revenue Department did was to take possession of land records. In those days, all land records were in physical form and anyone could manipulate them and claim ownership. By taking control of land and revenue records, the Government could avoid multiple complaints and legal issues at a later date.

If there is already a crisis and if you are part of the team to handle and diffuse the situation, you have the role of a curator than a preventer. A friend of mine encountered such a situation, where one of the branches went up in flames and got burnt partially. Fortunately, there was no loss of any life nor important documents, but the accident left the premises seriously damaged and affected customer services for many weeks. He made a list of priority works to be executed immediately. Some of them were the listing of damaged documents – especially customer-related, verification of any damage to the lockers where customers keep their life savings, restoration of power supply, reverification of electrical and systems networks, and assuring and rebuilding customer confidence. A support system was also provided to the branch immediately. In these situations, do not get carried away by the under preparedness of the staff, who have no clue about what can go wrong. Or they may be overreacting, leading to more panic situations and delay in restoring normalcy. In such situations, depute someone who has the experience. Assess the situation by viewing videos or photos. If things do not improve, visit the place, understand the situation, and then handle it.

But after a few days into the situation, if things do not improve in spite of confirmations from the staff, take the plunge yourself. In any crisis situation, the big learning is not to rely on anyone but to involve oneself. It is not to distrust your staff. Even they have no idea how things will unfold. If you are a leader and in charge of a crisis, you must be there at ground zero and handle/guide your staff. As the captain of an army unit, one cannot sit in an air-conditioned room and guide the soldiers to fight. Do not get carried away by either the negative or very positive responses of your staff, as they may have never faced such a crisis in their life. Crisis situations are not day-to-day affairs. There can also be a tendency in a few overenthusiastic staff to give a better picture than what the reality is. Some may have a habit of creating panic. As a leader, provide them with confidence. Pacify those who panic and handle the overenthusiastic team professionally. Share your experience with everyone and document it so that it can be of great use in the future.

Be careful about those who make a mountain out of a molehill. They create a crisis that does not exist. They make a small crisis situation look big and then create an impression that they worked hard to resolve it. In banking and many industries, there are more than one regulator and for many, the staff names of the regulators come in handy. Those in compliance and the legal team tend to take extreme views and convert small issues into major crises. While it is critical and important to be 100 percent compliant, creating a crisis for every small issue is a waste time and energy. And the 'missing the obvious' theory will apply – where people will miss out the most important and critical compliances when they are made to treat every small issue as a big one.

Some react to newspaper articles or some negative remarks on social media. We have billions using social media, which is unregulated. It is impossible to have any control. The only way is to keep tab of the negative comments, connect with them, resolve the issues and publish your revert on the same social media. Do not ignore the negative comments. At the same time, do not get hijacked by your staff who may make a mountain out of a molehill and create a crisis that does not exist.

Many organizations handled the recent Covid-19 crisis brilliantly. Apart from developing applications that allowed people to work from anywhere, they also ensured that they sent enough preventive and curative measures. Some organizations even arranged treatment in good hospitals and arranged the best possible medical facilities. At the same time, they kept tab on those who could misuse the liberty and freedom given. This helped in winning the hearts of the staff, who wholeheartedly worked for the organizations. If you see the quarterly results of many companies for June and September 2020, you will see hardly any impact of Covid-19 on the top and bottom lines, as staff rose to the occasion and delivered sterling performances.

Town halls

These are organized to address all the staff members in a location. The staff strength can be from 100 to 500 plus. These are organized when regional heads/country heads/CEOs/MDs/board members visit the location. These town halls in some organizations are also used by HR departments to create awareness about various terms and conditions associated with the job, to address new recruits, to inform about new HR initiatives, to create awareness on laws related to whistle blowers, the company's sexual harassment policies, etc.

The town hall is very critical and extremely useful. However, it can also be used to mislead, project something that's not real, and send a feel-good factor. The town hall must not be allowed to cook someone's career progression, to cover any lapses, or to project something that is not true.

The first feel-good factor that must be checked is the cut-outs and banners, various welcome hoardings, posters, and advertisements that line up from the airport to the venue of the town hall. I saw a huge rush in one of the airports. We witness such large crowds whenever a minister or a cine star arrives. Here it was the CEO of a company. There were a few senior staff along with close to 100 plus staff who came with garlands and welcome placards. The CEO was welcomed in a traditional way. There was a rush to get selfies too. Is this not a tripping point?

One will also see elaborate backdrops with background screens running the image of the dignitary. Then one will see nicely clad MCs kick starting the event. There will be plenty of staff who give a grand introduction of the person and some will narrate the dignitary's various achievements. No doubt, these are needed for the staff as well, as many may not know the great achievements and accolades won by the dignitary. Then comes the grand announcement, which is no less than inviting a cine actor. This is followed by the crucial testimonies and the Q and A session.

In Q and A sessions, staff are selected, questions are selected, and the staff are planted at crucial places in the town hall. In some organizations, they even have a dress rehearsal. Questions are given to the staff – who will ask harmless questions like the future plans of the organization, how do you plan your day, who motivated you when you started your career, why is the competition so scared of you, and so on. This is done because, as a leader, you do not want to hear anything unpleasant. Whether it is a pleasant or unpleasant experience, one need not take it as a litmus test and conclude that the whole region is like that. One person giving the best or worst feedback need not represent the whole organization. As a leader, take both of them with a pinch of salt. One need not doubt positive feelings expressed by staff, but one should not get carried away as well. One wrong incident or negative testimony need not be taken as a correct representative of the whole region. In such cases, a leader must take the feedback in the right spirit and come up with a solution. Also, take steps to ensure that the top management addresses such issues.

One must also note that we have a herd mentality. If one staff talks well about the organization, the rest of them will also do the same and vice versa. I was fortunate to work for an organization where such acts were never witnessed.

Those who succumb to such feel-good factors will lose 90 percent of the battle against mediocracy. One must remember that those who are performers and who work for the organization do not indulge in such acts. They also care and do not spend money on such personal worships.

In many FMCG and telecom companies, town halls are organized for dealers and distributors. During my initial days in Hyderabad city in India, I used to commute to my office using the local train service called MMTS. Early morning at about 8.10 am, I would meet regular officegoers who were from other industries like IT and telecom. One of them was working with a leading telecom company. He was busy scanning through papers and also making calls and he looked tense for a day or two. After a few days, he looked relaxed. When I asked him the reason, he said that he was part of the organizing committee for a town hall scheduled for his new CEO. He then told me how each and every aspect was taken care. He had gone to the southern state of

Kerala, where the previous town hall was organized. He had collected the details of the sequence of events, the likes and dislikes of his new CEO – including whether he prefers a carpet or a wooden floor in his hotel room, his preference for cars to commute in the city, his favourite food items/drinks, and so on. He had also studied the gist of his talk, the questions he had asked the staff and distributors/dealers, etc. In Kerala, they had not invited dealers/distributors who had a lot of complaints about the products/services offered. They had selected staff and distributors who would not complain and who would ask very good questions that would create a positive impact. They were all made to sit in different places in the auditorium to scuttle any suspicion. They also listed out pain areas already identified by the CEO. All these were taken care. Obviously, the CEO left the venue with loads of feel-good factors and the best possible memories.

I have a friend working in a major IT firm that has its head office in USA. They do not have a very strict hierarchy. They address every staff member by their first name. They are pretty informal. But they leave no stone unturned to ensure the smoothest possible visit and town hall to any visiting dignitary (and they need not be CEO or MDs but even their senior VPs and executive directors). Apart from managing the town hall and reviews, as mentioned earlier, they go one step ahead. They include a visit to local tourist spots, food joints, music shows, etc as a part of the itinerary. One of the CEOs was keen on visiting orphanages and old age homes. They had arranged for the same. Some like to have homemade food like idli, vada and dosas, which are South Indian delicacies. They would select a staff member whose family members prepare the best possible South or North Indian dishes. Their homes were refurbished and the dignitaries were taken there.

One CEO loved it if his staff did pranks on him and his immediate subordinates. They made elaborate arrangements to carry out pranks. They hired an agency to get professional actors who did the job. And this was done as soon as the CEO landed in his official jet.

In one organization, the CEO was made to believe that he looks like the Indian film star Salman Khan. A few went ahead and convinced him to enter the town hall in police uniform and dance to the tune of a very popular Bollywood number from Salman Khan's film *Dabbang*. The famous dance using the police belt was rehearsed by the CEO for many days and the event was a grand success. This act successfully wrapped up underperformance and many lapses of the company under the carpet.

Some get an advertisement inserted in the local newspapers and keep the copies on the dignitary's tea table in the hotel room and office. Their town halls will also have a staff member asking a series of questions to the visiting dignitary. These questions are supposed to be picked randomly from all the staff who write and drop the questions in a drop box. Even these questions are rigged. As we treat our guests as Gods, we also have the habit of giving a small memento. This will not be small – both in size and money. If you get carried away by such antics, you will demean yourself and, above all, the staff members lose faith in the entire system.

At the end of the day, the boss goes home happily. I am sure I need not explain in detail how one can take few simple steps to avoid pomp and glory and get the best out of town halls.

In addition, one must make note of the following points:

Some leaders have the habit of taking credit for all the good work and blame their staff for the failures and lapses. A true leader will take the blame for failures and appreciate the entire team for the successes. As a boss, one must know which category of people work for you and train, coach, and counsel them to adopt true leadership qualities.

If you are in the habit of listening to people far below in the hierarchy and also believe that whatever comes first to you is true, you will end up diluting the entire chain of hierarchy. One must always get skip level feedback and also use HR to get feedback from the front-end staff. Instead, if you believe that everyone who knocks on the door first is right and build your own prejudiced opinion, your one downs will start making dossiers about non-performing staff in order to protect themselves. They know that if they do not create enough records against the staff, you may encourage and support non-performers. They will also make efforts to deny the due credit for the good work they do, out of fear that it may further enhance their image and make it difficult to take action in case of non-performance. The best way is to keep your eyes and ears to the ground, give enough liberty and freedom to your one downs, and at the same time collect all the data and information before taking any decisions.

CHAPTER 3

Connecting Points: The Digital World

In today's digital world, we connect with staff through emails, messages, conference calls, and video calls apart from meeting them in brick-and-mortar offices.

These are the most typical modes of communication between you and your team. These are also the most cost effective and best ways to connect with people. Here are some tips one must use as a leader to avoid many tripping points.

Emails

This is now one of the important means to connect with your team. Most of the messages, approvals, etc, are conveyed through the emails. Information, circulars, new rules/regulations, memos, complaints, and even intimation of holidays is done through emails. There are several ways your subordinates can try to create an image which is not a reflection of their true self.

Please share an email etiquette process with your team. Every organization will have a clear policy on mail management. There will be rules and regulations to deal with while sending emails to external email ids dealing with customers, suppliers, regulators, tax authorities, government agencies, advocates, courts, and so on. There are mail etiquettes to be followed in each of these cases. Like in letter writing, even in emails, there are formal/ informal patterns. While dealing with government organizations the communication must be formal. For example, one cannot address them by their names. One has to mention their position and designation. In MNCs, some of them address their MDs with a single name, which may not go down well with other organizations. There are formal training courses and staff who handle external emails must undergo these trainings. Even when you deal with people within the organization, one must know when to use formal/ informal modes of communication. Please share these details with your team.

Mail traffic management: In many regulated sectors – like banking, insurance, and mutual fund industries – email traffic is heavy and at times unmanageable. One needs to plan and prioritize mails so that one attends to them as per their importance and criticality.

Some staff have the habit of calling and alerting you to approve an email even before they send one. Many times, it is to give an impression that the person is working very hard and is desperate to get things done. Please check whether it deserves the attention that is being projected. There is no need for anyone to call and alert to approve a routine matter. One must also communicate to the team that in case of regulatory issues and crisis situations, one must not hesitate to call and get the approvals. But for routine and mundane work, if someone is calling and drawing your attention, please be careful.

In many sectors, especially the service sector, one may get plenty of mails on product, marketing campaigns, alerts, complaints, compliances, escalations, approvals, success stories, etc. Some are to be read more than once, some to be archived, some are to be shared with staff, some mails are to be forwarded and followed up for action, and some are to be appreciated. At the end of the day, every mail should get its due credit. Most of the staff would use email for various purposes, as mentioned above. But many would also use it for creating impressions that are not true.

Some have the habit of sending emails for the work they do. Many times, the same success story gets published by many people, creating an impression that a lot of work has been done. Sales staff in a seed industry – who are supposed to do advance booking of seeds – would send a minimum of three to four emails on the same deal with different subject matter. As a boss, if you are not careful, you may get an impression that multiple deals have been done. But in reality, it is just one deal.

A friend of mine working in an insurance company narrated his experience to me. He had a staff who would call and inform him after he convinced a customer to buy an insurance product. He would send an SMS after he collected the initial premium amount and documents. He would send an email after the case got converted after due diligence. For a business of Rs 2,00,000, multiple messages through various channel would make it appear as Rs 8,00,000 worth of business. He would use the same tactic for every business sourced. The human brain recollects the latest event or events that are hitting it every now and then. A well-known Bollywood singer and music director composes songs where the same words gets repeated several times in the first few minutes of the song, with a very good rhythm and background score. Many industry experts attribute his success to the repetitive use of the same word and tune. It's better go by the facts and MIS.

Late sitting is an art and science for some, and for many it is due to lack of planning, time management issues, lack of delegation, and upward delegation by their subordinates. However, some people make sure to do all mundane and personal work through the whole day and walk in with so-called 'critical work' at 8 pm. Please be aware of this.

If you have any staff sitting in an office situated at a distant place, and interactions are far and few, please check what kind of work they do. Does it need late sitting? A friend of mine working in an office narrated this incident to me. He had a senior colleague who would never be in office the whole day. At about 7.30 pm, he would pick up a file, which he has completed by noon, and walk to his superior's office, which was located at a distance. He created an impression that he was so hardworking and sitting late, but the reality was different.

I normally used to end my day by 8 or 8.30 pm in my stint as senior VP in a private bank, though the branches used to close by 4 pm, and anyone sitting beyond 7 pm was considered late sitting. HR would alert the seniors on the late sitting menace by checking the network of the branch or transactions done after 7 pm and also by checking CCTV images. Many branches used to have some genuine issues and would take prior approval for late sitting. But some staff had made it a habit to sit late. Some bosses believe that whoever sits late is extremely hardworking, committed, and very loyal to the organization. So even after 8.30 pm or the next day before 9 am, I would have some 50 plus mails. I had sent several plans of action to avoid late sitting. I also resolved some system-related issues and helped them to streamline all operations after 4 pm. Yet I would get mails from late sitting staff. I also highlighted some staff who had received mails for seeking some approvals from me at 12 pm, but branch heads would be forwarding their recommendations to me at 8.30 pm. I sent an office memo and insisted that those who send mails after 7 pm must send me details of the work done by them on an hourly basis for the day. From the next day, I did not get a single mail after 7 pm. The point is that once you start questioning them, reprimand those who send mails at odd hours, and also help them streamline their work to avoid late sitting, the habit of sending mails at odd hours – just to create an impression – would end. People will not take unwarranted pain to create an image they do not have.

Many staff would seek approvals for various exceptions. They had to send the details through the mails. They end up sending lot of information that is not needed. At times, they would miss the most critical information. In order to avoid this, create a bullet point format for seeking approvals. The format must cover every important parameter but should be to the point. This will save everyone's time.

I used to get plenty of approval emails. In spite of sharing the format, many staff would not cover many details. They would just seek approvals. In a most regulated industry like banking, you may not get all the facts of the case, nor will you have time to seek more information. So I had developed standard formats that would cover every critical point that is needed to take a suitable decision. Be it single name approval, opening of accounts with some deviations, retrieval of documents, submission of documents to the court, etc, I had developed standard approval formats which would not only cover terms and conditions of approval but also guide the staff on what further precautions they must take.

One more precaution to be taken while handling emails is that you should read every mail. Do not assume just by looking at the subject matter and ignore them or delete them. Some have the habit of running through the mails without knowing the contents. As a boss, your accountability will not get diluted once you approve without knowing the contents of the mail. You know delegated powers for approvals, especially when it comes to approval of costs or offers to the customers. You cannot approve beyond your approval authority and it will land you in trouble. Letters to be sent to customers, regulatory bodies, police, customs, courts, etc, must be read carefully. Consult compliance and legal teams and your seniors. Do not just forward emails sent by your staff. The buck stops with you.

Messages

Today, most of the messages are exchanged through SMS and WhatsApp. There are many ways staff use these mediums of communication to put dust in the eyes of their supervisors.

Most of the organizations encourage creating groups with a common purpose to communicate with one other. Even important messages are sent using SMS or WhatsApp. If the number of staff in the group is more than 50, it becomes chaotic, and multiple exchange of messages makes it a very complex web from where one is expected to extract the information and act on it. Many times, series of messages exchanged get delinked when some unrelated information is exchanged. Like in the case of emails, here too, people use the platform to create an image they do not possess. Again, multiple messages are exchanged and photos shared only to create an impression that a lot of work is being carried out. A few send an important newspaper clipping related to the organization or business.

Another painful area is confirmation of work being done by each member to the head/boss. Once an important message or a directive is sent by the leader, there will be 50 plus messages confirming that they will comply. There will be few staff who would be eager to send the first confirmation. Most of the bosses tend to agree and believe such gimmicks and end up forming a good or bad opinion. While one must encourage staff to share the activities done or any success stories, please keep an eye on the actual performance. Those who may not be sharing such images but actually delivering far better results will end up being ignored. As a true leader, one must go with the facts and not get carried away by messages.

Conference calls (con-calls)/audio bridges (ABs)

This is another channel through which messages are conveyed to multiple staff at one go. These calls are usually used to convey an important message to all the staff who cannot be met at short notice. The number of participants in a conference call could be five to ten. If there are more than ten, the call will end up with frequent dropouts and disconnections. In case of audio bridge, it can have over 500 participants.

Many con-call and audio bridges are scheduled at short notice. Please avoid doing that; instead, give sufficient time. Fix the agenda and the total duration of the call. Keep last five to ten minutes for a Q and A session. Many times, a con-call is arranged to drive a specific product or to convey some important information. While most of the participants will hear, they will not listen and implement the directions given. Many staff will not participate at all. They will not have any MIS to talk about. Make sure that they come prepared and do not remain mute spectators.

At times, you may receive emails or messages from the mobiles of staff who are on con-call using the same mobile. Please take note of the same and warn them. So many will type the mail and keep it in the draft folder and send it after the con-call. One of the reasons is too many con-calls on routine matters. During calls, give them targets that they have to note down or assign a specific task that they have to execute. In the next call, ask them to update the progress. This will help you engage them and also help in making con-calls more meaningful. You may also ask some staff to repeat what was discussed. In most cases, 80 percent of them will not recollect what was discussed. One can also ask one of the participants to send the gist of the con-call. Otherwise, it will be a waste of time.

One problem in con-calls is that many times many staff members get dropped out of the call due to network issues. One should have a standard practice to follow in such cases. The best way is to call the leader – who can merge the dropped out calls.

Audio bridges are the most effective way to reach out to almost every staff in the organization, even if the numbers run into lakhs. These are to be used rarely – to convey a great news like 25 years of existence of the organization, major organizational changes, announcing milestones, new initiatives, etc. Do not use audio bridges for reviews and presentations. No one can see the MIS. Most of the participants will not understand what's going on. They just keep doing their routine jobs. Q and A session in such calls would be painful, as many participants will keep calling and asking same kind of questions or raise some local issues that have no relevance to others.

Do not have too many audio bridges too frequently. I visited a client in an IT company. He was on an audio bridge, but still called me into his cabin. Noticing that he was on a call, I gestured him to carry on with his work and informed him that I would wait or come some other day. But he put the mobile on silent mode and told me that it was a routine audio bridge and he had to be part of it as his boss was conducting the same. With earplugs in his ears, he discussed business with me. He took me to the cafeteria, and we had green tea. On the way back to his meeting room, the audio bridge ended.

While you may think that you had a great audio bridge, in reality many will not listen unless you conduct an audio bridge once in while on a specific topic that is very useful to them. And you must master the art of holding the attention of your staff for a long time. You need to develop a sequence, start the conversation with a few examples that are interesting. You must have a continuous flow of thoughts, modulate your voice, use examples and anecdotes, use humour, and conclude the AB with a great motivating statement.

Video calls (VCs)

VCs are the most powerful tools to connect with staff located in different geographies. Effective VCs can save travel time and money for the organization. VCs can be used for effectively communicating important messages, following up of key events, announcing major milestones, and reviews.

When VCs are connected with multiple locations, the screen size would be very small. Many staff make sure that the camera is zoomed out to ensure that they are not clearly visible. Make sure that you connect with relevant people, know what to ask, and whom to ask. Many times, this planning is not done. People ask someone who is more visible or more vocal. So it makes participants reduce their image on the screen and they will not open their mouths so as not to make any unforced errors. Those who are visible and vocal get hammered.

Many of them again try to talk about something that is not part of the agenda. There are many ways to hijack the whole VC by giving information about some critical news. Some take up help items, which are crucial but belong to other verticals who are not part of the VC. Some staff hide behind other staff members in a group and keep meddling with their laptops or mobiles. Some pretend as if they have received an important call, go out of the VC room, and return after a long gap. One must make note of this and control such behaviours.

When you schedule a VC, inform all the concerned staff well in advance. Share the objective or the agenda. If it is for a review, it must have scope to review what was discussed in the previous VC, what progress was made, and some lessons and takeaways. In most of the cases, including reviews, it's like a new movie. At times, VCs are called for some purpose and the participants end up discussing something else. In some cases, it deviates from the topic or revolves around some local issues, which have no relevance for others.

Invite only those who are needed. As a country head in an FMCG company, if you want to have a VC for all regional heads, call only them. Here some regional heads may call their one downs to have a large gathering. It's also to create an impression that they attach so much of importance to your message. Many people get carried away by such gestures. It also restricts you from taking some of them to task in front of their subordinates. Many times, when people at far lower levels in hierarchy join the VC, they always come with extremely high expectations. They have their own best possible impression of the top management. If the VC ends up in discussing mundane and routine jobs, the staff will start downgrading their image of the top management. In one of the IT companies, top management was discussing elaborately crucial steps needed while servicing their key clients. While discussing this, it was evident for the staff down the line that the top people had no clue about what actually was needed to service the clients, as they were handling the job and knew far better. So, it's better to know the job well before discussing it with your staff.

Ask the staff to get MIS and information needed for the VC in advance. Share the presentation so that they can download it at their end. Otherwise, they will deny the MIS, especially when they have underachieved. They will also dispute the MIS and say that they will get back with right MIS – and that will never happen.

Involve every participant in the discussion. If more than three to four staff members are hooked to the VC in each of the multiple locations, they mute the line and start discussing amongst themselves. Some will mute their lines and do not even look at the presentations and get into animated discussions. If you corner them, they will say that they were discussing a court case or loss of critical business and so on. They can be asked to go out and attend the same rather than distracting the entire team.

Make sure that the presentation is visible when you are beaming it. The MIS table in the presentation will be small. At times, they do not use the right font size. They link to some MIS, which may be too large, and they start searching for the specific MIS. Please avoid such issues.

Some more precautions to be taken are listed below:

While hooking on to multiple locations, make sure that an IT team member is there at each location to take care of the quality of the VC. Many times, the locations do not get connected in time. In some locations, they drop out and no one in the room knows how to get connected again.

Many times, visuals or audio, or both will not be clear. Clubbing a VC with an audio bridge creates confusion and disturbances. Please ensure that these are taken care of. Many participants do not mute the lines. There must be a standard protocol to be followed for all VCs.

Another necessary evil is serving water/tea/ coffee/ snacks during the VC. If VCs are for hours, it is understandable. Even for VCs that are scheduled for 15 to 30 minutes, as soon as VC starts, you will see neatly clad office staff coming with water and snacks. After five minutes, they will come and clear the plates. In the next five minutes, tea or coffee is served and then they again appear to clear the cups. Every time, one can see staff talking to them, making a few gestures, ordering some other stuff and, at times, they spill the tea, coffee, or snacks. The entire purpose of thus VC gets diluted. If the VCs are for over an hour or two, it is better to give a break and resume, rather than seeing these multiple dramas in multiple locations.

Do not indulge in a discussion that needs lot of time and requires support from other departments. Any topic that needs more time for discussion must be taken offline.

Complete the VC within the time allocated. Share the minutes of the VC with all the participants. The minutes of the meeting must have what was discussed, what the action plan is, who will execute it, how, and by when. The schedule for a follow up VC must be discussed and tentatively announced.

CHAPTER 4

The New Lens to View

As the head of the business vertical at a regional/zonal/national level, one must know what type of people work under him/her. While there are many ways of leadership styles like authoritative, participative, parental, and so on, it's better to know the different types of staff working under you so that it helps you to use one or more types of leadership styles to lead and manage them. It is impossible to fit all people into specific categories since, by nature, human beings are heterogeneous. This classification is based on what the contribution by the staff is and what it means for them to work. I classify staff under the three following types:

Those who work for themselves

Those who work for the organization and themselves

Those who work for the organization

Those who work for themselves

These are typically smart, at times over smart staff, whose main goal is self-interest. From day one, they work for themselves. If you peruse their biodata, you will see that they are not loyal to any organization for more than two to three years. If they are within the same organization, you will see them hopping from one department to another. They will have excellent links. They always scan the next best opportunities to grow both within and outside the organization. They use their stay in the department or organization only to build their career. They showcase ten times more than what they actually achieve. They are too smart. They are extremely good at presentations and drafting mails, and have the gift of the gab. Many a times, they act as trouble shooters. They are never loyal to the people who groom them nor loyal to the company. They are extremely greedy and power hungry.

It starts with the objective setting, Key Responsibility Areas (KRAs), or sales target setting in case of core sales job.

They will build up a case to first negotiate targets. They will come with well-documented information or MIS to go for lower targets. If we have a weak leadership, they even threaten to resign. You may come across a person in an organization who will sulk, show signs of depression, and even threaten to resign – only to bargain and get the targets reduced. It will work for them as long as the boss is vulnerable to such antics.

Some try to barter targets in a different product. In some organizations like banks, the appraisal system covers the number of branches achieving targets under a particular product. These smart people make sure that one or two sets of branches get the highest target under a product and the rest of the branches and locations get the least targets. It helps them to ensure that a maximum number of branches achieve their targets. Some organizations will have a weightage given to quarterly performance. So, they load all the targets to the last quarter to ensure that three out of four quarters, they overachieve their targets and get maximum benefit.

Most of the organizations have a set of rules to arrive at the next year's targets. They shall be a percentage over and above the previous year's achievement or the previous year's target – whichever is higher. This may result in punishing those who overachieve and set lower targets for those who do not do well in the previous year. There are many permutations and combinations while setting targets. It's always better to take into account the location, scope available in the market, performance by competitors in the same location, etc, and arrive at challenging yet achievable targets – where those who perform do not get punished and those who don't, get rewarded with lesser targets. Unfortunately, target setting in many organizations do not carry any fixed set of rules; instead, they are often arrived at after brainstorming sessions. In many cases, they get delayed for months. In some cases, other stakeholders will have to give consent, and that delays the process.

Backend operations teams need to be equally well equipped. For example, in banking, unless backend processing centres for cheque books, cards, IT, phone banking divisions, HR, credit, operations, and recovery teams are not in line with enhanced targets, the whole system collapses, leading to blame game, interdepartmental fights and, above all, leaves the front-end staff in the lurch.

In a prominent IT company I was associated with, the sales department went ahead with the acquisition of new clients aggressively, without creating a backup support system for servicing the client. Once a new client is acquired, one needs to provide IT support to them from day one for smooth operations. What happens if you have no resources to cater to them? In order to have a smooth client relationship, one must also build equally important support systems. While backend departments must have manpower in line with front-end departments, one must be careful while hiring people. In one of the IT companies, the department head scaled up manpower from less than 100 to some 1000 plus in no time. He created various departments under him and many more sub departments. Each was headed by a department head followed by managers and his staff. He increased his job only by hiring people under him and, in reality, there was no value addition.

Manpower management, especially attrition of staff, is the key criteria. If more staff resign, more negative marks will be given in the appraisal. If staff are asked to go or are fired for fraud or compliance issues, such attrition is not considered. These staff would make every resigned staff under the ATG (Asked To Go) category so that they get full marks in spite of poor handling of staff.

Those who work only for themselves never tolerate any second line of thinking. They are weak and immoral with limited capabilities. They will not allow smart and better abled staff under them to flourish. They will make them toe their line and create enough negative vibes about them if they try to be extra smart. They will not like any feedback or new ideas and suggestions.

They will use every possible way to project themselves as the best leaders. They will borrow ideas from all quarters and project them as their own. Every success story is owned by them. People under them have no option but to praise them on every possible occasion.

They promote only those who always say, "Yes Sir/Madam" for everything. They build a coterie around them. Since they will have set of loyal and obedient soldiers under them, they will be successful as well. In the short run, they become very successful, but the organization loses many talented people.

In case of non-sales departments, these people project their work as the best, most complicated, critical, and time consuming. Another issue in most of the organizations is that if you want a bigger job size – both in sales and non-sales departments – you need to have more manpower under you. Even for trivial issues, they take the shelter of regulatory bodies and create an impression that, but for their timely intervention, things would have gone wrong. Those who do not know the work at the ground level could end up believing the same. They would not have time and patience to understand the situation. They make very big vision statements. They roll out grand plans and try to add more departments, even if they have no value addition. They come with jargons, create task teams to monitor the work – all of which looks great. They create new hierarchy and get approvals with ease as they always quote some serious issues that may dent the image of the organization. While the top management always advocates reduction in several verticals, leaner organizational structure, automation, realignment, or removing excess manpower, they fail to see the sinister designs of these selfish people. Many times, they take the shelter of customer care, regulators, statutory compliances, best practices of competitors, advice from leading consultancy firms, etc, and end up building their own empire.

Some also look around and see if they can hijack and merge other units to make their own unit bigger. It's like inorganic growth within the organization.

In many cases, some of the top management team loses their touch with the front-end staff, whether it is sales or non-sales related.

Please give respect to the feedback given by customers and also staff working at the lowest level. They know the reality. Please try to know and understand every department, every job done by the staff at the lowest end of the hierarchy under you. Listen to a cross section of the people and not just a few of them. Meet the front-end staff directly and understand the job they do. Meet them from many locations and different geographies. Please do not generalize their opinion. Please check if they are only highlighting one-off cases or genuinely narrating the concerns and issues they have. One must also check whether the feedback given by them is not doctored by their immediate superiors. Check what support they need. Check whether work can be automated.

While creating new departments, check whether they are needed in the first place. You may see some staff giving a new name to an existing department. But in reality, it will be the same department that was dismantled few years ago as it was not serving any purpose. But in order to have a job size and to build their own empire, they create new units with fancy new names.

For every new manpower needs or departments, let there be an independent body along with HR to discuss and come up with a proper organizational structure. One must be very careful if someone comes with some fancy names for new departments. Please check whether it is necessary.

As a leader, the sooner you identify this category of staff – especially at top and mid management levels – the better. These are like termites who will affect the very fabric of the organization. One will also notice that the day they come to know that you have come to know of their sinister designs or the day they get far better and higher opportunities in other organizations, they will ditch and drop you like hot potatoes. If they stay with the organization, one will end up losing staff who are the actual pillars of the organization.

In order to deal with these types of staff, make sure to cut them to size as and when such manipulations are noticed. Have one-on-one conversation, even if one is a 'Man Friday' for you, and you make your intentions clear. Give them professional feedback and make sure that they work for the organization and keep their personal aspirations at bay and execute plans only in the larger interest of the organization. In most cases, either they will change and mend their way or quit. If they do not change their behaviours and also do not quit, one has to take tough decisions.

Another pitfall in fast growing organizations is the increase in the number of layers of management or hierarchy. Well, this is necessary and very much needed. But too many layers will end up in too many top/middle management staff making the same statements to people at the lowest level. Multiple layers of management will also dilute the intensity of communication. By the time the communication reaches the last person who actually executes the work, the information gets completely faded. Rapid growth of an organization also results in multiple departments. In most of these cases, many departments claim credit for the success. Interdepartmental movement of staff and assigning them the right responsibility with the right hierarchy will be the biggest challenge. Those who only work for themselves will tend to hop from one department to another, keeping the next level in mind. As a leader, you should cut unwarranted layers, merge multiple departments doing the same job, and create a far better and leaner organization.

Recently I met my cousin who works for an MNC company specializing in IT products. Over the years, the company grew by leaps and bounds, and as mentioned earlier, many layers and departments got added. Now the gigantic company is feeling the stress of its size and slowing down like an elephant. The new CEO who took charge recently did the first best thing one can imagine. He met every department head one on one and asked some very simple questions: What was the geographical area of operation, the names of important clients, and dates when they met them personally. Some were based in on the east coast of USA but handling west coast geography. Some could not even name two important clients. Those who named them had not met them or connected with them for years. All these group heads were given marching orders.

Some issues are in built and some are the creations of consultants. They come with new creative names, they come with vision statements for the next 20/30 years, they give some MIS which is generated by data analytics and AI (artificial intelligence). That's it. In no time, you end up hiring dozens of specialists and industry experts at an exorbitant cost. They will never show that their work is actually simple and easy, as they are the ones with the highest salary, perks, ESOPs, and bonus running into millions of USD. They use the art of making extremely impressive presentations. They create their own coterie, hire huge number of staff, and create their own empire. By the time you blink and open your eyes, they are gone. Never get carried away by consultant reports and never create new departments or layers unless they are absolutely necessary and are inevitable. Treat every department as a Strategic Business Unit (SBU) and get the cost to income ratio (CI). Stop multiple departments sharing the income for the same deal. Keep the doors open for feedback. Have interdepartmental committees and ensure that they work as a team. If anyone works only in the interest of oneself or one's department – at the cost of the organization – show them the exit door. Have ways and means to spot such people and ensure that you get rid of them very soon. Be careful about these people, as they always create tripping points for leaders.

Those who work for the organization and themselves

These staff work for both the organization and themselves. They find a way to confluence the objective of the company and themselves. They will not just work for themselves at the cost of the company. They are sincere.

They manage their work very well. They bargain for their targets reasonably with logic. They try and get the best team. Their manipulations do not harm others. They also manipulate, but to a lesser extent. They do not take risks. They take up assignments that are new but interesting. Unlike the first category, they do not form a coterie around them but get carried away if anyone praises them.

They do not care much about their targets and promotions. They try and bargain. If it happens their way, they are happy. Otherwise, they are fine. But given a chance, they grab with both hands.

They do not manipulate to get the best locations with the least targets. They are capable of managing tough staff members and tough locations if the management reposes faith in them. They highlight their work once in a while and do not always indulge in a self-canvassing fete. They may quit the organization if they are side-lined or the company promotes and encourages the type one category staff.

Though they are fairly harmless, one must coach and guide them. They need to be groomed for the next level. They can be trained to acquire the mindset and skills required to go to the next level.

Those who work for the organization

The third category is a rare breed and endangered. These staff own up for the organization. They always put organizational interests first, rather than their professional/personal interest. They are real Karma Yogis.

They never negotiate targets. They just do not get involved in target setting. They never bargain, and never try to manipulate target-setting exercises, as explained earlier. In fact, they do not look at MIS and realign their strategies. They just breathe, think, and walk for the organization. Most of the times, they end up taking on more targets and higher responsibility than others.

Unless they are ill-treated or disrespected, they do not quit the organization. They never desert the ship when it hits turbulent waters. In fact, they take charge of the ship and navigate it safely. They seldom quit the company. They respect the management's decisions and move from one department to another only when asked to do so. They do not ask what is in it there for them. They do not create hype. They will not keep knocking on the door of management asking for salary hikes, the next promotion, etc. They believe that recognizing talent is the responsibility of the company. They do not indulge in office politics. They never build network to take advantage for personal gains. They never tolerate anything negative about the company. They give frank and unbiased feedback, which may be construed as arrogance. But as you know, truth is always bitter and no one likes it. In the world of sycophancy, honesty becomes the victim.

As a boss, do not burden them with excessive targets. If you are a keen observer of human behaviour, look deeper into targets versus actual performance. Avoid getting carried away by the hype people create and you will not miss these people. Be fair to them. Check what kind of locations they operate from and compare their performance with others. Look for granular growth in business. Those who only work for themselves manipulate even their small achievements. In many retail organizations, they end up taking a few bulk deals at the fag end of the year and overachieve their targets. Some organizations have a process of knocking off such bulk deals while setting targets for the next year. They take advantage of such loopholes and end up over-performing and also getting lesser targets for the next year.

Another proof of the existence of such staff is that they do not negotiate and bargain on the locations they handle. They take up the most challenging locations where getting manpower is tough, the market is limited, and there are many logistics issues. The cost of reaching these locations is always higher than in metro and urban locations. But they take up such challenges and deliver reasonably good results. Many a times, organizations fail to recognize their contributions. If you travel once to these locations and understand their hard work, you will not ignore these staff.

The last and most critical factor is manpower management. They always end up taking staff who are mediocre, at times dumped by other departments. But they don't crib. They love mentoring, coaching, and handholding staff. They spend considerable time in grooming their staff and motivating them. This takes a toll on them. As mentioned earlier, they do not build a coterie around them. They will be tough on staff who have integrity issues, especially those involved in sexual harassment cases or frauds and would never try to protect any staff who violate the extant guidelines of the organization. They do not cheat even a single rupee from the organization nor leave anything due to them unclaimed.

They are happy with the ratings they get and do not care much about promotions. They would feel bad if manipulative and undeserving staff get recognition and they are overlooked. These staff are the pillars of the organization. They do not ditch in times of any crisis. They stay loyal and work hard to build the organization. They do not just look at bottom/top lines and dance to the tune of investors. They also take tough decisions and never compromise on their moral values.

As a leader, one must possess the art of spotting such people and then preserve them. They are not flamboyant, flashy characters. The biggest mistakes most of the top management team make are that they want everyone to be more energetic, exhibit leadership qualities by smiling for every silly joke one cracks, hide negative stuff if any and always say "yes" to whatever is told, and never ever ask for any help or suggest anything which is worth looking at. From the pick-up at the airport until they are dropped back, one wants to see and feel only good things. In today's times, it takes no time to manage this. It can be a welcome poster at the airport and hoardings all along the road to doctored, stage-managed town halls – everything can be arranged. Unfortunately, this rare breed of staff does not indulge in such acts. Negative character is to see negativity in everything. But these staff want to have more improvised products, processes, share the best practices of competitors, and try to bring changes that are long term and good for the organization. Many times, their valuable suggestions are stigmatized as negative characters and they get side-lined. As mentioned earlier, "Truth is always bitter," and real leaders always bite it.

If their professional life is made hell in every possible way, they start showing signs of stupor. At times, they start detaching themselves and, in a worst-case scenario, they quietly resign and disappear from the scene. But they would never badmouth the company and people. One must spot such staff, listen to them, have the courage to bite the bullet, and groom them to lead further. In reality, these staff are the maximum contributors to the organization. The 80:20 rules apply here as well.

CHAPTER 5

Deception Management

Deception is an action of deceiving someone with wrong representation or through misinterpretation. It's tricking someone. I remember a game played in India, especially in rural areas, and now there are national level tournaments. It's called 'Kho Kho', where an entire team chases one person who needs to dodge and keep escaping. If any member of the chasing team touches him/her, he/she is out of the game.

The same happens in the corporate world. There are some staff who are adept in deception. Unless one is alert, one will not be able to even gauge that one is being deceived. And there are reasons why some staff indulge in deception. If you take care of the following weaknesses, you will not get deceived.

People will deceive you when you are:

Wrong

Unreasonable/unrealistic

Passing on what you get from your boss

Unaware

Prejudiced and have false assumptions.

Too strict or too slack

When you are wrong

Being wrong is not being correct under a set of circumstances. As a boss, you are supposed to be fair and right in your judgements and decisions. You cannot afford to be wrong, as it impacts the people and the organization.

One may make wrong judgements. If you have not created an open work culture where people can politely give feedback, they will continue to nod their heads no matter whether decisions prima facie are wrong. It can happen when you do not have the full facts of the case and depend upon a coterie of people who are ready to put the dust in your eyes. Over dependency on a set of incompetent people and advisors can lead you to taking wrong decisions. In many situations, there is nothing right or wrong. Only time will decide whether the decision taken by you was right or wrong. If you have a consultative approach to problem solving, no one will deceive. If you elaborate the reasons behind your decision, they will buy it, as many staff under you, may not have enough experience nor would they have the full facts of the case.

In a few cases, you may have to take an opinion from legal/compliance teams and take a decision. Please ensure that the people who implement the decision also know the full facts of the case. But, in most of the cases, people take impromptu decisions that are wrong and non-starters from day one.

Smart leaders can sense this by the body language of the people around. I have seen some smart leaders who can read between the lines when the responses are sent through mails and messages. Many times, in an autocratic management style, no one ever gives any feedback.

When decisions are wrong or perceived to be wrong, the only way staff react is to deceive. They give fake reports which cannot be cross verified. They also send exaggerated scope to get business in the future, which no one will cross verify. They also fail to implement the decisions and come up with fake results which cannot be verified. They send reports that lack facts.

It is better to have people who are sincere, honest, experienced, and can give honest feedback. They must also be given a pilot project to dipstick the decision – if there is a scope to do so.

When you are unreasonable or unrealistic

An unreasonable and unrealistic boss is the one who has no clue about what he is asking for. I remember in my college days, a very strict administrative head made it mandatory to conduct theory classes for one hour and practical classes for exactly three hours. In agricultural science, you have classes spread across 1,500 acres of

A Leader's Tripping Points

land and classrooms are usually half to 2 kms away. Some practical classes get over in an hour and some may take more than three hours. The new rule was a non-starter and yet it was ruthlessly implemented. This led to chaos and confusion and finally to a prolonged strike that affected all the students.

A friend of mine joined as an officer in a public sector (PSU) bank in 1997 and narrated this incident to me. In his first two months, during a rush hour, his manager called him and handed over a huge sheet and asked him to complete it and submit it by the end of the day (EOD). My friend had no clue what it was. After he could get time, at about 7 pm, he saw the format and it was the budgeting sheet and was to be submitted for the next year on a monthly/quarterly basis. He promptly asked his colleague, who said that it would take a minimum of three to four days to complete. My friend went to his manager and told him that it would take three-four days. The manager blasted my friend and asked him to complete the task the same day and reminded him that he was still under probation. My friend was hurt. That day, he completed his part of the budgeting exercise and submitted it to his manager. He also told him that he worked for the bank and customers and that he had never thought that one could relax after the probationary period was over. He informed him that the planning sheet had come from the regional office 15 days back and was lying in his own drawer due to his own negligence and that the last date to submit it was over. He also told him to connect with the rest of the departments to get the task completed. The next day, the manager called my friend and expressed regret for his outburst.

The point is that if you are too unrealistic and unreasonable, your staff will try to deceive you. Another way for my friend was to fill in whatever figures came to his mind and place it on his manager's table or divert his attention to another major issue – like a court case or a major customer complaint – and shrug off the responsibility. He chose to tell him the truth. It is better to be realistic and reasonable when you give a task, set a target, or come with a plan of action. It must be challenging yet doable.

In some organizations, they set sales targets which are impossible to achieve. In FMCG companies, they compare the performance of a competitor who has double the sales staff and networks than yours, and yet they want you to be number one in sales in the same geography. They keep setting benchmarks that are next to impossible. In some organizations, goal posts keep changing and formats for appraisals are very tough and they change the parameters midway. This makes it very difficult for the staff to shift their strategies. They will then start deceiving the system or they give up.

The most important unreasonable/unrealistic expectation is to expect every staff member to perform better than the best at a pan India level. If someone in Hyderabad has sold 100 water purifiers in a month, all staff must sell 100 purifiers. If he can, then why not others? It is always good to compare with the best performing staff and encourage others to follow the best benchmark. But it must not lead to demeaning the staff. We deal with human beings. It's not like putting one ton of raw material to get 1000 units of end products and then put two tons to get 2000 units. There is a need to come up with positive reinforcement rather than negative. I can say that I successfully adopted this strategy when it came to my zone's performance. Though we cannot compare between any two zones, as they are spread in a different geography, manpower strength is different, scope for business is different, and yet I set the highest benchmarks. I could come up with a brilliant plan of action after eliciting a response from my team and I created teams with team leaders who would track the performance. We encouraged everyone irrespective of how much they contributed. The targets were made simple and doable – provided they implemented many of the strategies we developed. The results were amazing, and we ended up among the top three pan India in specific products month on month.

When you pass on what you get from your boss

If you are in middle management, it is very easy to tell your subordinates that you got the instructions from your boss and hence this must be done. The positive part of it is that it gets its due attention and people take it seriously. It also drives home a point that it is needed at the top level and hence critical. But the negative aspect is that once you start firing by placing the gun on the shoulder of your boss, you lose your credibility. You will have to depend upon your boss or boss's boss to get your work done. If you respect and own up to your boss and believe in what he/she says, you will also have better conviction to persuade and convince your staff. In many cases, people criticize their bosses openly. They are at loggerheads with them all the time. They do not convey the message from him with all the seriousness it deserves. In all such cases, people down the line will resort to deception.

In order to have a buy-in from the staff, you must inform them about how critical the task is. Top management will always have a larger perspective and take decisions as part of the grand design. The strategies are part of the master plan or a vision for the organization. The front-end people may not even gauge it and will not have a complete buy in unless it is explained to them as to how critical it is for the organization and in turn for every employee.

Many times, the staff do not even understand when someone says that super boss has asked to do something and hence do it. They will never implement such orders with heart and soul, and such directions either end up in complete failure or get stuck after some time.

Use the boss's name sparingly. Inform staff as to how every decision will help them first, then the customers, and then the organization.

When you are unaware

When computerization was introduced in PSU banks in the late 90s, most of the trade unions opposed it. The front-end staff refused to use them, fearing that it may end up in job losses. When they were made to understand the advantages of computerization, they started using computers slowly and steadily. Today, all PSU banks and government departments use the latest cutting technology, and using laptops is now a way of life. Automation and computerization got integrated in every organization.

As a supervisor, you must be aware of the decisions you take. You must also be aware of the problems you may face. I have come across plenty of situations where the boss is completely unaware of the problem on hand. They fail to gauge the implications as well. I also had an opportunity to work with bosses who would anticipate issues in advance and avoid them completely or give multiple solutions to handle them.

Being unaware is due to lack of experience or lack of paying attention. In all these cases, it is better to admit the ignorance and learn. I have worked under a boss who would first say, "I do not know and I want to learn and you guys explain it to me." That was brilliant. In many cases, the boss, in spite of being unaware, will end up asking, "Please look at this work, complete and submit." Here your staff know that you know nothing and are unaware. They will deceive you either by giving wrong information or will demean your position by sharing it with the rest of the team.

Please be aware of the issues on hand, understand the product, process, market, or customer and then delegate and take decisions.

When you are prejudiced and have false assumptions

Prejudice is a preconceived opinion that is not based on reason or actual experience.

Prejudiced and false assumptions emanate when you want to hear only the news that pleases your senses. Anything bitter is considered as negative, rebellious behaviour, and pessimistic attitude. If you exhibit such a style of management, people will deceive you in hundreds of ways. They will first dissect your behaviour and understand factors on which you take decisions. If praising you or your kids, your dress sense (how so ever bad it may be), your speech, your sense of humour, etc, makes you happy, then God bless you. There are people waiting, watching closely to discover what are the reasons that will force you to have a favourable opinion of them. That's pretty easy to make out. They will find out how and when you praise a person. When you praise a staff member who has done very well in selling a product or was first to send a compliance to a new process. Here one must closely watch the information given. Many times, a mere visit is made and an agreement with a client or a government body is signed. It doesn't mean that the company got the business or that the advance amount has been received. A detailed customer visit report is sent only with promises. If you keep praising such acts, the rest will follow, and that's easy for the staff to do so. In some organizations, especially banking, there shall be multiple channels targeting the same customer. Here also one does his best to prove that one was the first to strike a deal.

Many a times, one instruction from you in a WhatsApp group would get positive responses like, "Yes Sir/Madam. Great idea. We will do it. Rest assured, etc." They will make sure that whatever may be the situation, they will say 'YES' and reiterate your instructions verbatim. This is because you have created an assumption that those who do not reconfirm are non-compliant staff. At the end of the day, actually those who have not sent a confirmation message end up doing better job than those who sent a message in less than five seconds of seeing the message – where it takes a minute to read the message. Your false assumptions will lead people to deceive you by sending a confirmation message.

Quite often, people depend upon what they see, hear, or read about someone first and then freeze the same in their mind. They never crosscheck or connect the missing links to decide judiciously. At times, they over depend upon the same coterie who have made a lot of efforts to get into your inner circle. You must have seen people connecting with personal assistants, drivers, or security guards to gauge the mood and then approach a boss at the right time. Most people fall prey to this. They never realize that there is a grand design being webbed to get closer to you and to win your confidence. They have ample time for these manipulations, and you might have seen them getting great success as well. But it is at the cost of pushing down deserving candidates who work sincerely, and they will either settle for less or quit.

In many cases, personal favours play a critical role in deciding whether a person is good/bad/ugly. No boss likes a person who works on his own, delivers results, and keeps a low profile. So people do not miss a single opportunity to showcase their talent. Giving personal favours is the most dangerous and most used weapon to create a favourable impression. While every organization has a strict code of conduct on acceptance of personal gifts, many ignore the same. It is also linked with the concept of great Indian hospitality. It is also important that one must respect and take good care of the visiting dignitary. So, one must be extra careful about the acceptance of gifts. Luckily, the organizations I worked in never had that culture, whereas many of my friends in other organizations and other sectors had a different story. There are a set of unofficial protocols for south/ north Indian bosses and foreign bosses. More than the official reviews, the entire itinerary gets hijacked on personal grounds. One may go home with lot of feel-good factors; however, it is nothing but getting deceived.

Expensive gifts, arranging a dance program, getting IPL tickets, etc, are some of the weak points people cash upon.

Opinions are a sum of a series of assumptions one forms about others based on what they see, hear, and read. It is better as a boss if you evaluate each of these stimuli, wait for the results, and then act, but never fall prey to the traps.

When you are too strict or too slack

If you are too strict or too slack, people will try to deceive you. One cannot be strict or slack on every deviant behaviour. One must evaluate whether the event/incident is compromising or uncompromising. One must be strict on deviations in regulatory processes, genuine customer complaints, sexual harassment cases, and so on, and can be lenient on some of the more trivial issues. If there is no such differentiation and one exhibits the same behaviour, one will get deceived.

Even in the case of uncompromising situations, before any decisions are taken, one must evaluate the event or situation thoroughly. These are most critical and sensitive issues, which need to be handled with lot of care and after a thorough investigation. Most of the time, top management will depend upon a few people who always give the wrong advice, leading to harsh decisions. Most of them are knee jerk reactions. This doesn't help at all. It is also superseded by very strict processes, which will be a major stumbling block in sales and also in servicing customers.

Too strict and punitive behaviour will result in denials, diverting attention to much more difficult personal or professional situations. If you are very casual about even important events, you would hardly succeed as a leader.

During demonetization in India, specific currencies were taken out of circulation by the government and people were asked to deposit the currency in banks within a specific period, leading to lot of cash transactions. This was basically done to curb black money and control the parallel economy. Many front-end staff ended up violating a few norms of the Reserve Bank of India (RBI). Many banks, fearing a backlash from RBI, went gaga about sacking staff members. These were the staff who were doing three to four times more cash transactions in both value and volume. Some violated the cash acceptance/exchange norms unknowingly and some did it deliberately and in connivance with the customers. A few banks were evaluated for such violations by independent teams and took a fair view and punished only those who had connived. But a few banks did not have the patience to evaluate and took harsh decisions, leading to more attrition of staff, reluctance of existing staff to manage cash counters, and staff taking extreme care in every transaction, leading to delays and customer complaints. Here, many staff resorted to deception and survived the axe. Those who were honest but violated the norms inadvertently got punished.

Some top bosses are always slack and turn a nelson's eye to every deviation. They do not take anything seriously.

They always try to protect the staff no matter whether they have violated processes that are uncompromising. This leads to further deterioration of the processes, more violations leading to frauds, decrease in staff productivity, and reaches a point of no return. More often than not, these bosses end up losing their jobs.

There are many deviations or violations that are not very serious in nature. They would not have any impact on the sales/service levels of the organization. While there is no need to take harsh decisions, one needs to keep a tab on such issues and warn the concerned staff as a series of deviations on small items will finally lead to big issues at a later date.

Here again, if you take harsh decisions, people will fail to differentiate between what is critical or non-critical. This confusion can further erode their decision-making abilities. Laws cannot be the same for the inadvertent picking up of a beetle nut to stealing an elephant.

I have come across, in many organizations, how some people end up being favourites of their bosses no matter what. They always show the highest amount of loyalty to every boss they work with. The whole world knows about their ulterior motives, except the boss. In the corporate world, no one indulges in direct bickering and they always use other, indirect means. These guys are the master manipulators. In a few days, they have an exhaustive list of manoeuvres to be made to grab the attention. Some are specialized and become 'Man Friday' for specific events. Well, each person has a weakness that is ready to be exploited. It is better if these weaknesses are kept to oneself.

CHAPTER 6

Skip Level Pitfalls

Skip level interactions are nothing but interacting with staff by skipping one or more hierarchies below you. These are done in most organizations. Many staff down the line in a hierarchy would like to hear from the super boss directly. It is indeed inspiring for them to interact with top management. These are important interactions but can be very misleading if proper care is not taken.

Skip level interaction is crucial for every organization. Some of the benefits are given below.

Disseminating management objectives

Skip level calls and meetings are necessary to directly disseminate important changes in the organization. It can be the launch of a new product, compliance to a new process or audit guidelines, or new policy changes which would impact the organization. If you directly connect with all the staff, it helps them understand the management's objectives better. These are also important when new management team has taken up the job or a new set of critical objectives or specific marketing campaigns are rolled out. These can also be used for disseminating important news items, crossing of milestones, or introducing key changes in the organizational structure.

For better impact and results

At times, you will have no time to take the new process through the hierarchy. In such situations, it is better to connect with the one downs and get quick results. It can be a revert to a regulatory body. In banking, it can be a pending foreign inward remittance or a revert to an external statutory authority like the police/tax departments, a court order, etc. This will help to get a quick response and one can revert to the concerned party as quickly as possible.

Open work culture

Skip level interaction is the best way to get a gut feel of the organization. Meeting staff helps to understand the work culture better. It also creates an open work culture and cuts the hierarchy. It helps a leader to connect with people and get to know their aspirations and concerns. A true leader will also spot whether people at the ground level are happy and highly spirited or not, even if they do not show their feelings.

Ease for new joiners

It also gives new joiners a sense of belongingness and helps them settle faster. Many times, they face a lot of issues when they join a new company. They take time to adjust to the new work culture. Check if they have got proper place to work, whether they have got a job description, ID card, email id, name plate, targets, etc. Check if they are aware of their terms of service, the rules related to the dress code, parameters associated with confirmation after the probationary period, their eligibility for various facilities, the process to move to other departments, the appraisal process, and the promotion policy of the organization. Share if there are any formats for the appraisal process and core areas that they need to focus on. Many times, they are not even guided to complete the joining formalities, leading to a delay in processing their first salary. All these and many more concerns can be addressed.

It also helps the organization to retain staff who at times get isolated and lost in the system, especially when one is working in a large, multi-departmental organization.

Skip level escalations

It helps staff to approach the next level in case there are teething issues that are not solved by the immediate superior. One cannot follow hierarchy in every situation. Many administrative related works do not get addressed at the local level. Skip level escalations help them address these better.

Skip level escalation must be done more vigorously in case an immediate superior is involved in frauds, favouritism, scandals, money matters with clients, dual employment, etc. These are very critical, and one must do skip level meetings to get the best possible information to solve the issue.

However, there are pitfalls one must avoid. There can be more harm than benefits if these are not handled properly.

Embracing more than necessary

Your interactions with junior staff must be for the intended purposes and not beyond. You need to interact and know them to understand the organization's culture and their expectations but do not let them sit on your head. Getting too close to them and embracing them more than necessary will make you prejudiced and vulnerable. You will start doing the work that is redundant and could be handled by the staff themselves or their immediate boss. You will end up with more upward delegation and thus ruin your own authority. They will start calling for promotions, better ratings, transfers, etc. This must be avoided.

Cuts the hierarchy

If you indulge in skip level interactions for routine works, it will rob you of time and energy. Too often, skip level interactions make your immediate subordinate's job redundant. Staff will have a tendency to make every small and trivial issue a big one to draw your attention and to meet or call you. Sooner or later, all the staff will make a beeline to meet or call you for every trivial job. It makes the rest of the hierarchy redundant. The staff will either tend to downplay it or allow more such interactions so that their work pressure comes down. They will also not be accountable for any wrong decision taken by you.

Gives an extra edge

Some bosses even tell their staff that they are the supreme authority and not to worry about their immediate superiors. They give an open invitation to come and approach them any time for any issue. This is the most disastrous way of managing people. It gives undue advantage to the staff below. They take not only their immediate superiors for granted, but the whole system. Some people think that skip level meetings are the only way to establish their superior authority in the organization. In reality, it erodes the same.

Chance to abuse the power

Frequent and uninterrupted skip level interactions will help them abuse power. This is the biggest menace in our country. I have seen how a clerk who is well connected would not even care about Class I officers in a government organization. They know that they are closer to power centres and can get away with. That's the reason why people cling to power centres. By encouraging this, one will create an organization that has a weak hierarchy.

Unwarranted upward delegation

Your immediate subordinate will tend to relax and give you an upward delegation. They may encourage their staff below them to approach you directly. A friend of mine had such a boss. Luckily for him, during one such incident, his boss approved a request sent directly to him, resulting in a major fraud. Since my friend was not in the picture, he was saved. It was a blessing in disguise. It's better not to take any extra load for no reasons.

It under develops your staff

Once you have a line of people waiting for you to get your audience, it leads to a situation where anyone could walk in to get his/her work done. They waste your time and energy. If your involvement covers routine transfers, hiring of staff at entry level, salary corrections, promotion at the lowest level in the hierarchy, early relieving of staff, rehiring of staff, and so on, it will not develop any skillsets for people reporting to you. They will not take any interest in their work as well.

If you want to grow further in the organization, you need to focus on your core objectives and also develop the people who report to you. The more they work independently and get results, the better. They also need to know when to connect with you and for what. Otherwise, you will stagnate in the organization along with your team and get into a comfort zone.

CHAPTER 7

Change Agent for Managers

It's a boon to have the right people working with you. I have worked with amazingly talented and excellent staff under me. They would work on simple directions. I did not have to blow my lungs to get the work done. Unfortunately, such breeds of staff are rare and declining. The challenge is to set clear benchmarks and change the behaviour of the staff working for you. Today, people have different aspiration levels. Millennials are brilliant and may not fit into the traditional work culture. It again depends upon the organization's culture, and your immediate supervisor. If he/she encourages skip level interactions more than needed or if he/she indulges in appeasement policies, it is unlikely that you will have any control. Here are some ways to handle such situations.

Get the BEST anyway

We do not live in an idealistic world. While you may not get the best staff to work with, there is no harm if you try to get the best out of them. As the head of the branch, I had very unique and yet diverse staff under me.

Some came from completely different geopolitical and cultural backgrounds. It was a challenging task. But I was well equipped to deal with people, thanks to my stint in Satya Sai College and their ever-inspiring teachers. I must narrate about Sri Satya Sai College in Alike, a small town 45 kilometres from Mangaluru, a district in coastal Karnataka. This college is run by a dedicated team of teachers who have sacrificed their lives for the betterment of education by coaching, caring, and inspiring thousands of students. I have learnt the best management principles there and hence am ever indebted to them.

So in a span of 30 plus days, I was able to get the best out of every staff member in my branch. I realized that each person is talented and has come to the organization to work and grow. What is needed is to know their strengths and weaknesses. Capitalize on their strengths, encourage them, and get the best results, and then work on their weaknesses. It can be on product knowledge, communication skills, people management skills, time management issues, etc. All these are acquired traits and can be modified by proper counselling and training/coaching. But one needs to have patience. However, deal firmly and assertively if there are any staff members with a negative attitude.

I have also come across a boss who would always encourage and get the best out of every one, no matter whether they were less capable. His words of encouragement and his belief in the team made them work better.

Over a period of time, if the staff do not come up to the expected levels and do not improve their performance, see that they move to a department where their skill sets are put to use. In any big organization, you will have many departments which can accommodate such staff. If this doesn't work out, it's better to ask them to look for a job in an organization in the same or different sector, where they can put their skillsets to use and prosper. Never keep on flogging a dead horse nor have an indefinite time frame to change people. This will ruin the career of the staff and your own performance.

Micromanagers and post mortem analytics

These staff are obsessed with micromanagement and miss the larger picture. You give them the task. They have 100 issues even before getting it started. Some take ample time to even explain to you what problems they may face if they adopt a specific strategy you suggest to them. Nor will they have any alternatives. They also take time to elaborate every task in a detailed manner, as if they are explaining rocket science to a kindergarten student. They send elaborate mails and messages to explain and seek an approval for a simple task. Some have the habit of giving detailed report on why a particular strategy failed. It's like a post-mortem. While it is necessary to analyse the reasons for failures, one cannot just keep on elaborating the same. If there is a failure of any product/marketing/advertising strategy across all geographies, it makes sense to analyse. Otherwise, one must implement the strategies, work hard, and work smart to get good results. As a leader, one needs to train people to implement first by putting in 100 percent heart and soul into it (as there is no single best strategy for any challenge), get the best possible results, and then come with a few takeaways.

I had the fortune of having such people. The best thing I did was to have a one-on-one conversation with them. I made my points very clear. I laid down guidelines when they spoke to me. I gave formats for seeking approval so that they would not send me irrelevant information or miss crucial points to seek approvals. The formats were with bullet points. Over a period of time, they fell in line and I got the best out of them. Please ensure that staff do not get stuck with analysis of a failed strategy. They must be made to move on.

Impatient and ruthless task masters

Some are born like this and some acquire these qualities. People with these qualities have no patience. They do not have the time to develop people. They expect everyone to know everything. They will have mastery in some skills – be it MIS management, product knowledge, or customer contacts. They will only tolerate those who toe their line and become callous or ruthless with those who do not. They never take feedback but are ruthless in giving negative feedback. Usually, they will have their own set of people and can be nasty even with them. They will have higher levels of attrition. One has to do a major balancing act here to manage them and the people reporting to them.

Once again, sit one on one with them and lay down your observations. You must give examples of losing otherwise good staff and subsequent business loss and complaints post their exit. You must teach them anger management tactics and draw a line without diluting their authority. Support your point of view with independent reports like an upward feedback report from HR. Performance improvement cannot be due to ruthless task tracking and constant pressure. In the long run it will not work, as people will stop as soon as pressure levels come down. Many will not like such a style of management and may leave, while some start finding ways to escape.

Docile and accommodative

Staff with these characteristics get their work done by putting a gun on someone else's shoulder. They will be too docile and accommodative. At times, an accommodative style helps to retain loyalty, but it also breeds incompetency and personal loyalty rather than organizational loyalty. But they will also have high degree of non-compliance and delayed reporting and lacklustre performance. They hate to take tough decisions. They will not even issue a memo for a major lapse. They end up creating a bunch of lawless staff below them.

Give them feedback with facts and situations. Give examples of staff who were performing earlier and now are laidback, as they were never tracked but accommodated. Being nice is okay but it must not build incompetent and lazy staff. I have seen a major transformation in some of my staff, who changed for good and are now great performers.

Master manipulators

These are born geniuses but use their talent for the wrong reasons. They always think selfishly. They make sure to use every possible information to their advantage. They are shrewd, intelligent, and manipulative. It doesn't take much time to recognize such talents. If they use their skills for the betterment of the company, they will grow and go places. But they will not give up their selfish motives. They always try to skip you and connect with your boss. They stay in touch with other verticals and look for lucrative opportunities outside the organization as well. They are loyal to themselves and never to you or the organization.

Another disadvantage of such people is that they get exposed sooner than later. If you are smart, you will spot them easily. They also miss the obvious. Too much intelligence will make them indulge in too many manipulative works. If they had focused on their task, they would be among the top performers. Instead, they manage MIS. They manage people at the top and are always restless. They can never be happy. They never enjoy life, as their mind always flickers to get newer and better things for themselves.

Make them understand that you have spotted their motive and know them well. Bring them back to organizational objectives and core goals. Be alert and do not approve their requests without cross verifications. Their approval requests need to be double-checked with facts before they are approved. Once they understand that you know them well, that you mean business, that you are a thorough professional and a tough nut to crack, they will be normal. Again, giving and taking a constructive feedback will be of great use.

No matter who works under him/her, a true leader will spot talent, coaches/grooms staff, gets the best out of every staff member, and makes sure that there is no scope for any manipulation.

CHAPTER 8

The Art of Managing Human Resources

Lead

If you know your area of operations very well and have all the data that is needed to take a decision, then go ahead and lead from the front. If one has a better conviction and belief in one's strategies, one must go ahead and implement them. There should not be any more delays once strategies are worked out. Plan your work and work out your plan. Even after analysing heaps of data or MIS and seeking advice from the best of the best consultants, there is nothing like a magic formula or the best solution to a given situation. More than that, it is the implementation of the strategy that holds the key to success. In any dynamic organization, there is no perfect or imperfect strategy. Have a conviction. Lead from the front and implement. If it works, fine. Otherwise, there is a lot to learn.

What to do it? How to do it? Who will do it? By when?

Any planning must have these four ingredients. It can be a sales strategy, process compliance or customer service excellence. One must first analyse all the facts in hand, get the relevant data, or consult an expert and decide what needs to be done. This must lead to some tangible numbers, like increase in sales/customer satisfaction, or product improvement, etc. It is also relevant in terms of how to do it. This step must have elaborate plans and alternate strategies giving an account of every step in detail. If it is sales, it should cover the top customer segment, customers who walk into the store, and a database of existing and new customers. It should cover proper product narrative, coaching of staff, proper monitoring, and course correction steps. Your plan must also have 'who would do it'? Many times, no one in the team is given the responsibility to implement the task. One needs to assign the task to every staff involved in the process. Again, it should cover top-end customers, walk-ins, and the database. Preferably, a team must have a mix of seniors, experienced people, and/ freshers so that it is implemented properly. There must be a review mechanism to check the progress vis a vis targets set. Here, as a leader, you must direct, advise, or counsel and take course correction decisions. Finally, your plans should never be an indefinite journey. All plans must have a target date where one must analyse the degree of success or failure of your plans. There are no wrong plans.

There will be a learning for you and your team members. If it is successful, document it for future use.

Stop the 'I know all' attitude

As a leader, one must never show an attitude of 'I know it all'. Anyway, it gets flattened in no time. Today, any kind of knowledge and skills can be acquired with ease. They are not exclusive domains of any sect. As a leader, you need to understand the limitations of your knowledge and skill levels and accept and learn. It will help your subordinates to open up and give you the much-needed information and data to take crucial decisions. If you are not open to new ideas and always show a know-it-all attitude, no one will ever share an idea with you, and you will be surrounded by ready to clap clowns around you all the time.

Do not let it affect your performance

When dealing with a few rogue characters more often than not, one tends to forget their core responsibilities. This may impact your performance. Please make sure that you get back on track. Many times, when you do not get the desired results, you tend to brood over the matter and you take tough measures, leading to more conflicts. Avoid the same and focus on your core objectives and performance. You must be unruffled irrespective of the outcome. After all, not everyone is borne to be successful in every aspect of life. In fact, most of us get carried away by success or brood on failures. Both will derail the existing performance.

Move on

You have enough subordinates to work, and you cannot afford to spend more than the necessary time and energy on one single person. Once you have a professional feedback session, deal with each situation and move on. The more you stay focused on one issue or person, the more you get dragged or tend to stagnate. Just move on. On the lighter side, if you are supposed to carry some ten monkeys on your head, see to it that all of them come with you. In spite of your best efforts, if some monkeys get down (due to their sheer nature), do not stop and start only when all monkeys are back on your head. Just move on. They may join you later. And if they don't join, it doesn't matter.

Keep it professional

People tend to discuss the behaviour of your team, either with one of the team members or with your colleagues and superiors. While it is better to keep your boss informed, do not discuss things with anyone else. Keep it professional. Many times, corporate offices become a hub of grapevine or gossip, lobbying points, and group-ism. There are no real and genuine colleagues and friends. Most of the time, it looks like an African safari, where you can see stronger/faster animals working out plans to hunt down the weak and or claim a new or lost territory. If there is too much attention to this type of politics, one will be bogged down forever. Please do not get into any gossip or political debates. Keep it professional and impersonal.

Keep it minimalistic and simple

Too much of talk, discussion, exchange of emails, ideas, plans, etc, lead to waste of time, mudslinging, cleaning dirty linen in public, and creates a bad environment. Keep your interactions as minimal as one can and keep it simple. This works in your favour.

Be assertive and polite

This is the most effective tool to deal with anyone. Give the facts of the case. Be very assertive but polite. Never use foul language and make unforced errors. Convey your points in simple, clear, and categorical terms. Set deadlines, record the same, and follow up. There is no point in using an assault rifle to shoo away a squirrel. Use the right force at the right time with not much noise. Many times, if you do not even react, the issues are settled automatically.

Give and take feedback

During the course of your interactions, make sure that you are open to new ideas and experiments – provided they help in achieving the core objectives. Giving and taking feedback is the best way to engage staff and win their trust. One must also be open to negative feedback and work on the same rather than being defensive.

Work on their strengths

Everyone has some talent in abundance. Some are good at public speaking, some at data crunching, and others in people management. While you must counsel them to work on their weak areas by arranging professional training, capitalize on their strengths. It gives them more confidence and gives you and the organization better results.

Ring fence yourself

We are all infectious. We spread good or bad things that we have, and we also absorb the same from others. It's natural and unintentional. You move in a group which has its norms, and you will get brushed with the same traits and later get soaked completely. Ring fence yourself against any of these odds and protect your core identity. Being part of a group is good as helps you identify yourself with the group and gives social security, but do not cross the boundary. There is an old saying that goes, "Good fences make good neighbours."

People spend more time with their colleagues in office than with their spouses at home. Many times, the thin line of keeping personal and official relationships apart fades. People rush to get into a relationship. After some time, the gloss fades and the relationship sours, leading to many allegations and counter allegations. As a leader, ring fence yourself. You would have seen several lawsuits against many top-level executives who ruined their career and reputation for indulging in illicit relationships with their staff and even customers. They promote them, give them contracts, and break every rule. These acts cannot be hidden. Many countries have very harsh laws. It also leads to the loss of job and reputation, broken families, and huge financial obligations. Attraction to people working very closely is the weakest point many leaders fail to resist. Many times, it can also be a tripping point. Many have made successful careers out of such acts, but the reputation of the organization and person gets eroded and it's a matter time before it engulfs the company.

Detach emotionally

You may have a tough time when you lose the best performing staff to competition. It's a terrible feeling. You would have invested your time and energy in coaching the staff and taken personal interest. You would have given every possible marketing tip and shared all your experience. The person would have learned the tricks of the trade and enjoyed career growth. You would have never imagined that he would ditch you and the organization for some more perks. It can be devastating emotionally.

Have least or zero emotional attachments with people around you. It is tough if you closely associate with your team. If you come across a person who has a matching wavelength, and have an absolutely delightful experience with them, you tend to get attached emotionally. But then, everyone has his/her own career plans, and they will tend to move on. Work professionally. Detach emotionally. Stay in touch with them even if they are not part of your team or organization.

Be positive and do not give up easily

There are times when you tend to give up and go for an extreme step of putting a person on a notice period or the exit list. Maintain a higher level of patience. Work on them repeatedly. I have experienced magical transformation in my team members. They turned out to be outstanding performers from their earlier mediocre self. A positive attitude is now a part of the placebo effect that is making the rounds in social media. This was mentioned in the ancient Indian scriptures thousands of years ago: "Yadh Bhavam, Tadh Bhavati." It means – what you think, so shall it be. If you think positively, things will be positive, and vice versa. In India, whenever someone speaks negative things, others always say, "Speak well so that good things happen." They do not want to even hear negative things. We worship every form, be it stone, people, animals, or trees and believe that they all have magical powers to heal and get us positive things in life. It is a part of our culture. There are instances where people misuse it to deceive gullible people, and some may call it superstition. At the end of the day, it is a positive belief that is reinforced by using some means. So be positive and speak, think, and hear positive things. Trust me. It works.

Do not overrate

This is a mistake almost all of us commit. There will be a bunch of staff who are always overrated (more than they deserve) in terms of their position, responsibility, salary/perks, and promotions. They may be great performers.

There is no point in going overboard. Please be cautious and extra careful. They will put enormous pressure on the system to get to the next level in no time. They expect out-of-turn hikes in salary or promotions and always try to be indispensable. Please set the expectations right and keep their replacements ready, as they may ditch you in no time. And my experience is that overrated staff will either ruin your image or take all the possible help you can offer and then quit to join the competition.

Praise in public, give feedback in private

As humans, we are impulsive and spontaneous in our responses. As soon as an incident happens, we react immediately. Stop. Think. Act. For all the good work, praise them in public. For bad work, meet in person or call privately and give your feedback.

Appreciate work but reward only performance

Some subordinates have the habit of working very hard with negligible or no results. Some pretend to work hard but are mediocre performers. Some spend the whole day on trivial issues and work late. Some create very good impressions. One must appreciate hard work and that's it. For rewards, one must get results. Please make people understand the difference and work suitably.

Manage expectations

Under promise and over deliver is the mantra for customer delight. The same applies to the staff as well.

Be it a salary hike, job rotation, promotion, or higher responsibility, make sure that you make a promise based on the company's policies, set expectations right, do a professional evaluation, and give a pleasant surprise. As one goes up the ladder, the number of positions will be much fewer. Salary hike and perks will be less. Make sure that these are explained in detail so that staff is not exposed to unpleasant surprises.

Be responsive

One has to win the trust and faith of every staff. You may have come across some managers not being responsive or helpful when someone need them the most. They tend to leave the most difficult situations to their staff to mend themselves. At times, responses are late, and they are as good as no responses. Please act and react fast. In many legal matters and regulatory issues, one must respond instantly and help them connect with subject specialists. Here you must (as mentioned earlier) have given enough freedom to your staff to call you any time to get timely help. There were instances in my career where I was called in the middle of the night for an emergency fire accident in a branch. At times, even personal matters of some staff need one's quick response. A staff called me once at 2 am in the morning to help him get O negative blood for his wife, who was delivering a baby. I rushed to the hospital, called half a dozen blood banks, and also staff member to help him. These are rare incidents but need a quick and positive response from you as a boss.

Keep subordinates at arm's length

You may have an excellent subordinate who is not only a great performer but also a great human being. However, keep at a distance as long as you have a boss-subordinate relationship. If you are closer than professionally needed, it will give ammunition to others to churn out rumours from the gossip mill. Even when the staff member gets his/her due credit for the performance, people around may link it to the personal bond you have with the staff member. At times, staff may also try to take advantage of the situation. Even if a staff member is professional to the core, better keep him/her at arm's length. If you become a boss to your own batch mate from college or even your seniors, have only a professional relationship. Avoid unwarranted personal rapport, which may harm both of you.

No credit, no blame game, but fix accountability

As a leader, you are responsible for the success or failure of your team. You need to own up everything. You cannot take complete credit for the success of your team. As a leader, you give credit to the team members for the success and take the entire blame on you if the team fails to meet the objectives. You cannot blame anyone – neither the team members nor any external factors for failures However, you must also identify key contributors in your team for the success and recognize their contribution. Similarly, you also must fix the responsibility and hold a few staff accountable – who did not show team spirit and did not perform well.

You need to do this when you discuss the matter with your team in a review. When it comes to reporting to your boss, you must take the entire responsibility.

Know your staff

In an organization, people join from many walks of life with varied socioeconomic backgrounds. One must know your staff, their lifestyles, and saving and spending habits. Many staff go through a very rough personal life. Give them a break and help them to manage personal issues first. It's very common to understand the family background of the staff you hire, apart from their educational qualifications and experience.

There are many informal meetings with the staff and their family members. In India, it is common to have family gatherings where one meets their parents/spouses, etc. There are mentor-mentee programs, which help staff members to express their issues to mentors, and mentors take time to help them. If one knows the issues staff have in their personal life and if they desire so, proper counselling can be arranged or professional assistance can be provided to help them. In extreme situations, staff end their life because of personal issues. These can be avoided if you know your staff. Once your staff perceive you as a thorough professional and a person with golden heart, they will open up and share their concerns.

I have come across people who help their staff to tide over their issues at home to get them out of depression. One must also not probe too much about a staff member's personal life. When one discusses issues with the staff in a feedback session, these concerns crop up, which can be resolved with due permission from the staff. Knowing their socio-economic background helps to know how critical the job is, how best the person is suitable for the job, how far a person can adapt, and so on. But in any official conversations, one cannot quote one's personal life.

Listen

This is the most important characteristic of a successful leader. We tend to know everything. We ignore people below. We do not even give a patient hearing and then decide whether the views/opinions of the people are good enough or not. One of the reasons for this is that we tend to have preconceived notions and prejudices. It may be true that subordinates will always come up with reasons and excuses. But only when one listens, will one know the facts. In many cases, they may come up with brilliant alternatives or ways and means to improve strategies for effective implementation. Even if you deny their views, they will have the satisfaction of having given their opinion. If one is not open to listening, then they will not come out with new ideas in future, and that is detrimental to the organization.

Do not have an urgency to disprove or argue with them

Most bosses come with a fixed agenda. They do not want to listen or take another viewpoint. Another reason is that they never try to improve any plans/strategies that they get from their bosses. They always say, "Brilliant idea, superb one, Sir. We will implement it." After accepting and appreciating, they cannot go back to their bosses if they realize later that the strategies were completely wrong. So, the best way to do this is to somehow argue or disprove anything that subordinates say. They will go to any extent to disprove any suggestion. This needs to be curbed. One must either convince the other person or get convinced. There cannot be a middle path.

No nonsense beyond a limit

Liberty, freedom of thoughts/expressions, newer ideas, etc, are all the best ways to get the best possible solutions to the issues on hand and get the best results. Too much of liberty or freedom may also end up in unlimited debates, discussions, and lack of commonality while implementing the plans and, above all, delayed response time. As a leader, one must get the views of all, analyse facts and decide a set of plans which must be implemented 100 percent. Any underperformance, arrogance, lack of team spirit, cold response to customer complaints, deviation from process compliance, etc, must be handled firmly. This must be made known to the staff as well. Any acts of insubordination, acts of violence against customers or colleagues, defiance to terms of service, acts of sexual harassment, etc, must be dealt with an iron hand, irrespective of their past performance. If one tolerates nonsense, one gets nonsense all the time. This also sends a strong message to the rest of the team.

CHAPTER 9

Conclusion

Genes, form the very basis of our existence. All our physical, mental, and emotional aspects are made up of the genes that we inherit. These traits are passed on from generation to generation. We not only inherit genes from our parents but also from our grandparents and great grandparents and so on. If you study genetics and breeding, you will know how complex and yet so simple the process of the birth of a progeny is. It's a miracle. It's the most complex creation one can think of if you look at the process scientifically and yet, it is so simple and natural. The human body is a magnificent edifice consisting of complex systems like the nervous system, digestive system, reproductive system, respiratory system, and so on.

Though it is a deviation, I would like to highlight the fact that we are all the most able and fittest people as of date, as we are alive and kicking. We have a history of a gene that is being passed on from generation to generation. Today it is unimaginable and surprising to know that just a few decades ago, diseases like plague and cholera killed people in tens of thousands and wiped out entire communities. Many floods, earthquakes, and famines have ravaged countries from time to time. Our ancestors roamed in jungles in search of food and shelter. They had to struggle to survive. Life was not so simple and easy thousands of years back. It was the survival of the fittest. They were fit and hence survived every onslaught on their life. If any one person in our ancestral chain had not survived before the procreation, we would not have been born today. Generation after generation, all were fit and healthy, and hence we are here and hence we belong to the fittest families.

From now onwards, how we survive, and bring up the family decides the future of our next generation. Since we carry loads and loads of genes in our body, we behave depending upon how specific genes dominate, resulting in exhibiting a particular dominant behaviour. Technically, all human beings have brains made up of the same types of cells, which have more or less the same capability. Still, heredity affects mental ability. Some families will have a history of creating great scholars, academicians, musicians, or sportsmen of great calibre. It's all in the genes.

However, one can change one's behaviour depending upon the environment in which one grows. The entire family environment is the result of the sum total of behaviours and the line of thinking of every member in the family. Neighbours influence us a lot in terms of our values and behaviour. At times, I feel we all live for our neighbours. We tend to compare one on one with all people we know, especially neighbours, and try to imitate them. There is nothing like the constant pressure being created by a neighbour.

In an organization, we assemble people from different religions and castes, and regional, linguistic, or cultural backgrounds. With complex gene structure followed by the influence of environment, these people will have to slowly and steadily get merged with organizational objectives. It is not an easy task. It starts with the recruitment of the right people for the right job. It involves proper and timely training, fair and unbiased target setting, impartial appraisal and promotion system, proper coaching, and handholding by supervisors. Creating a great work environment doesn't mean providing swanky offices, work from home facilities, highly employee friendly policies, equal employment opportunities for all, and so on. They are essential, but it also involves spotting and nurturing talent, lateral hiring, a systematic, unbiased appraisal system, and steady growth of the organization along with the growth of the employees.

Creating a conducive and better work environment to house people of different ages and experiences, different skillsets, and varied religious and linguistic backgrounds is the job of a leader. Too many rules will make it like a military base and too much of slackness will end up in chaos and indiscipline. Respect for the law of the land, a fair and challenging job description, respect for values, ethos and professional behaviour can be created and nurtured by well laid out terms of service. In addition, the organization must also create a work environment where favouritism, prejudices, and biases are extinct and only merit, humanity and professionalism exist. The promoters and the top management must lead by example and walk the talk. They must set highest possible standards, lead from the front, and ensure that every person in the organization imbibes the same work culture. Once this is created any newcomer – be it a fresher from college or an experienced lateral hire – will easily merge into the existing system. They will absorb and perpetuate the same work culture.

As mentioned in the beginning the idea of this book, my objective was to ensure that as a leader you are not taken for a royal ride. Pooling my 26 years of corporate life, after my interaction with hundreds of staff in several organizations in various sectors, I have compiled tripping points people create to trip their leaders. I have also offered ways to build a great organization by developing people, as they are the most important but complex resource to manage. A leader must not have any weak point, as everyone observes the leader, and they cash in on the weaknesses. They say, "One must see as if one has eyes all over the body and one must listen as if one has ears all over the body." A leader must see what others normally fail to see and read the situation. A leader must listen to what one normally doesn't say and take a suitable decision. After all, every single decision can turn to be good or bad and may end up in the success or failure of an organization. As a leader, you must ensure that your contribution is not just sales, increased market shares, unprecedented top or bottom line, but also building a future leadership team, creating a robust work culture and a blame-free environment, a loyal and delighted customer base, and leaving a legacy that is unprecedented.

I am sure you have enjoyed reading this book as much as I enjoyed writing it. You must have come across some of the tripping points I mentioned in the book. If not, I am sure, sooner or later, you will come across them in your career. Have a great leadership journey devoid of tripping points.

www.ingramcontent.com/pod-product-compliance
Lightning Source LLC
Chambersburg PA
CBHW030801180526
45163CB00003B/1118